Here is all You Need to Know About

Funding a College Education

The Parents' Job is to Save

The Student's Job is to Get Good Grades

Surviving the Cost of College

Revised Edition
2018 - 2020

Bob Sherman

North Cove Press
PO Box 213
East Greenwich, RI
northcovepress.com

ISBN Number 978-09995436-2-7
Library of Congress Control Number 2018903131

10 9 8 7 6 5 4 3 2 1

Surviving the Cost of College, Revised Edition
is also available as an eBook at Amazon.com

Written by: Bob Sherman
Edited by Martha Reynolds

Photos and Cover Design by Bob Sherman
Contact the author at: bobsherman.net

Dedication

This book is dedicated to my wife Lisa, for without her support, the revision and updates made in this book would not have been possible, and to our daughter, Catherine, who is attending Worcester Polytechnic Institute, providing fresh insight and understanding to the college experience.

Contents

Chapter One

My Practical Daughter

My practical daughter plans to become a microbiologist studying human genetics with the hope of saving the planet, even though the earth (rocks and shrubbery) is not made up of human genes. Knowing that college is expensive, and she needs money for the final push (a Ph.D. and post-doctoral work in genetic transmutation engineering, if I understand her correctly), she has decided to attend an in-state school that is far less prestigious than those chosen by her peers. It will cost us only $15,000 a year. She further decided to reduce that cost by attending a community college for the first two years with a tuition rate of $3,000, before transferring to the frowned-upon yucky school. My daughter's four-year Bachelor of Science degree in microbiology will cost the family a total of $36,000.

So, my question to all the parents reading this is, "Do you have a son or daughter this practical?" Neither do I. That's why I began searching for financial solutions to pay for college that resulted in this book.

As a parent of a college-bound student wondering how I could afford to pay for my daughter's higher education, I spent what seems like forever looking at the factors that increased and decreased our eligibility for federal and private aid. I'm more optimistic now than when I began and believe there is hope for us all. Financial adjustments can be made, and financial strategies can be employed to increase college aid, even in September's last dark hour before filling out the Free Application for Federal Student Aid (FAFSA). For those who plan a year or more in advance, the options are considerable and the rewards significant. By the way, don't say you are filling out "the" FAFSA. That's akin to saying you use "the" Google. It makes you sound like a doofus. Just ask my daughter who's going to save our planet.

My journey began and ended in the same place, FAFSA land. The government's free application consists of about 100 questions that you answer online. Many of the questions are answered simply by clicking a yes-no box. The immediate benefit to filling out FAFSA is learning where the government sees you within their conspiratorial schematic of presumed ability to pay for college. This is a know-thy-enemy, know-thyself paradigm, the first rule in the art of war and negotiation. FAFSA is also the Khyber Pass to federal dollars, state dollars, institutional dollars, and student loans. Without a Passport (AKA the FAFSA-generated Student Aid Report), you can't get into the country.

Because the purpose of this book is to provide the information needed to develop a plan to pay for college, we've deconstructed and analyzed the federal formula to show how each of the four components relates to the expected family contribution in the eyes of the federal government and the college financial aid office. We have also provided a substantial list of options to increase college financial aid.

FAFSA is a multi-billion-dollar federal umbrella of grants, work-study, and student loans managed by the college or university financial aid office. They mix these parts into a simmering cauldron, add the eye of a newt, and produce a Financial Aid Package for students after they have been accepted for admission. (The simmering cauldron is actually a college computer loaded with federal formula software. Like I said, the eye of a newt.) While the computer grinds away, you may receive an acceptance letter in January or February, then have to wait a while longer before you receive a financial aid package, making the final decision a nerve-racking affair. Now let me take a step back.

I appreciate that some parents are reluctant to fill out FAFSA. Some believe they earn too much money to qualify for federal aid, and many parents don't want their children or others to know their family's financial position. Both reasons are understandable, but think about this: first, your AGI (adjusted gross income) would have to be in excess of $150,000 not to be eligible for some aid from private colleges that cost $65,000 or more each year. Second, colleges and universities provide millions of dollars in private grants and scholarships based on

the student's grades, SAT scores, and athletic and artistic ability; but before they give up a dime, the finance office will want to see the student's passport.

With regard to the privacy of your finances, your college-bound student can go online and fill out the student questions in FAFSA with or without supervision, then close out the application. You can log in later to enter the family's financial information, or you can answer all the questions yourself. I expect my daughter to answer her share of questions since she's the one who gets to go to college. Filling out this form will also provide critical practice for her future world of employment and visits to the doctor's office. I will check her answers, however, to make sure she did not mistakenly click yes to any of the questions in section three, making her a runaway homeless Iraq veteran with children.

The idea for this book began with a few parents discussing how we could afford the cost of our sons and daughters spending four years having the time of their lives, while they earned a degree in something we may never fully understand. The suggestions were as varied as the number of people sitting around the campfire. In this book we cover every legal suggestion that came up, plus a few that are borderline just for fun. This book is a continuation of the campfire discussion. So, get something to drink, sit down, and read what we have learned.

Now a word about saving money and using this book.

A friend of mine has a two-month-old baby girl. He stopped buying expensive coffee in the morning on his way to work and instead buys coffee at a convenience store. This saves him $2.00 a day which he puts in a container and eventually in a bank account. He plans to save $2.00 a day for 365 days each year, or $730 a year. In eighteen years, when his daughter is ready for college, he will have saved $13,140 without the slightest amount of sacrificial belt-tightening. This is a true story, and when he told me, I was incredibly impressed and told him so. He didn't understand why it was such a big deal. It's a big deal because there are people at the other end of the spectrum who think they can't save and won't bother trying. People who put themselves before their children and this frustrates the hell out of me.

There are many financial vehicles described here that you can use to save for college. The only one I would recommend to you is not on the list, and that is saving $2.00 a day.

There are many options for you to discover in the book, laid out for your viewing pleasure in an open field. Just remember, they are options, not recommendations. Every person lives within a unique financial circumstance and must make decisions based on their situation. I'm taking you to the top of the bluff to look over the grassy plain. Look around and see what's there. I don't recommend you shoot the buffalo or mess with the Indians. If one of the financial instruments or financial strategies strikes your fancy, talk it over with a financial planner or someone you trust, then decide. This is exactly what I told Custer, but he didn't listen, and you know what happened to him.

Postscript: Since the first edition of this book, our daughter is now a junior at Worcester Polytechnic Institute studying bio-technology and is on track to finish her degree on time and jump right into graduate work. Because she is in the field of science, we expect our financial role in her education to decrease, unless our government decides to decrease its role in funding scientific research.

Chapter Two

The Cost of College

The cost of sending our children to college has become a major burden. It is not only college that has gone up, but the everyday expense of supporting a family has increased to a level that often requires the financial contribution of both parents. This was not the case in the 50s and 60s when one parent could support a family, and a student could pay a large portion of their tuition with the proceeds of a summer job.

The cost of a four-year college can be anywhere from $20,000 to $69,000 a year, depending on a number of variables, including in-state and out-of-state rates, private vs. public colleges, non-profits vs. for-profits, federal grants based on income, college scholarships based on merit and unique talents, the goals and needs of a college to maintain the characteristics of a defined student body, and the student's willingness to serve in the armed forces.

How do you manage all these variables? In the end, how much you pay depends on how early you begin to plan.

You can estimate the cost of college for your children in the future by multiplying today's tuition rates by 3% for every year between now and the day they begin decorating their dorm room. If you have a child in grade seven, the cost of today's tuition could increase by 15 to 20 percent by the time they receive their acceptance letter.

How does the cost of college stack up against the rest of our economy? The Bureau of Labor Statistics reports that between 1980 and 2014, the cost of all goods as measured by the Consumer Price Index rose 120 percent. During that same period, the average cost of college rose 260 percent. The cost of public universities went up 296 percent and has continued to rise by 2 and 3 percent every year thereafter.

Where does that money go?

First, very little money goes toward faculty salaries. The American Association of University Professors released a study that shows during the last seven years, salaries of public-college presidents and senior administrators rose 11 percent on average, compared to 7.2 percent for professors. In addition, colleges and universities use part-time contingent (adjunct) instructors who often work more than one job to earn a living. Contingent faculty make up 40 to 60 percent of college instructors today.

Benjamin Ginsberg, professor of Political Science at Johns Hopkins University, in his book, _The fall of the faculty: The Rise of the All-Administrative University and Why It Matters_ (Oxford University Press), provides data showing that between 1975 and 2005, administrative positions have grown 85 percent, and associated professional staff has grown 240 percent, while faculty have grown only 51 percent.

During this same period, the number of students has grown from 9.6 million in 1975, according to the Department of Commerce Bureau of Statistics, to 17 million in 2004, according to the National Center for Educational Statistics. Today, approximately 20 million college students are roaming campus quads and filling up classrooms. About 880,000 of the best and brightest, by the way, are from other countries.

How do so few college instructors accommodate so many? It is not unusual for 150 or more students to be herded into a lecture hall for Biology 101 or other required subjects during their first and second year of college. My next-door neighbor used an electronic clicker synched to a university software program that registers her class attendance when she walked through the door. The professor may never know who she is, but a computer located in the basement of the building knows she showed up for class.

It is also not unusual for students to spend five or more years in college, because the required courses are not offered every year, causing them to delay graduation while you write more checks. At this very moment, my daughter is carefully selecting her courses so that she will be able to take the required classes in sequence without losing a semester between offerings. Careful planning and management of college coursework is crucial to finishing a degree in four years. Typically, less than 50 percent of students graduate from public colleges and universities in four years.

So back to the money. Where does it go? Have you visited a college campus during the summer and noticed new construction or buildings closed for renovations? Schools are in competition with one another to provide the most aesthetically pleasing dining rooms, athletic facilities, student unions and libraries, and a Wi-Fi infrastructure, all designed to wow the prospective student. While the cost of new construction is not paid with your dollars, the cost of operations and maintenance is thrown into the general budget, which is absolutely funded with your tuition increase. Most colleges offer students counseling and academic support, free tech support and employment services, except they are not free. The cost is just buried in the school's tuition and fee structure.

And last but not least, why do colleges charge so much for tuition? Because they can. Higher education operates on a free-market-basis. As long as there are more applications than available slots, tuition will continue to go up.

.

Chapter Three

Preparing for College

Message for Parents

Creating the best possible financial position and collecting the information needed before filling out FAFSA online can be a daunting, time-consuming and lonely job, but we are not alone. Twenty million students are expected to attend 4,500 Title IV eligible colleges and universities, with costs ranging from $20,000 to $65,000 per year, totaling more than $60 billion in tuition, room, board, books, and an assortment of fees you would have never guessed existed and had to be made up on the spot when their balance sheet tilted toward red. Eighty-five percent of these students will receive financial aid through the Higher Education Authority, which means you and I are poised to fill out the Free Application all alone in front of our computers along with seventeen million of our closest friends.

The good news is that **billions of dollars are available in financial aid** to help pay for college. The bad news is that those billions are divided among millions of students, leaving a lot of college costs left over. The Federal Education Budget Project reports the government has $30 billion in grants and one billion in work-study grants available. This is the side of the table you want to be sitting on. They also have $99 billion available in student loans. This is the side of the table to avoid if possible. We have some suggestions, short of abstinence, if you begin planning early.

Sixty-two percent of all financial aid is offered by way of a loan. Student debt exceeds a trillion dollars and has become a major financial crisis in this country, spawning new industries willing to consolidate loans for fees that only increase the debt problem. I don't consider borrowing money from the government at higher rates of interest than my home mortgage to be financial aid, but I'm not the government, so I don't understand these things. And by the way, weighing your sons' or daughters' potential servitude to the banks against the financial value of their future college degree, though painful to your college-bound student, is well worth your time. Putting aside for a moment the idea of following your heart, some degrees are more valuable than others in the marketplace. Calculating your Return on Investment (**ROI**) is always a worthwhile Exercise.

College Selection
Yes, the student selects the college, but the college must select the student in return. Our sons and daughters send an application to the college admissions office where it ends up in one of four baskets. They have different names, but all mean the same thing. They are: Sorry, We'll See (Wait-Listed), Yup, and Grab-This-One-Quick. The admissions office mails out an acceptance, deferred or rejection letter.

The amount of time between applying and receiving an acceptance letter can be a month or more, creating a period of anxiety greater than that caused by waiting for the SAT scores. With today's technology, you would think colleges could find a way to shorten the time. How about one day where students visit the campus with their records, receive an interview, go on a campus visit, and before heading home learn whether they have been accepted; you know, like Unity College in New Hampshire.

If your son or daughter is accepted, the financial aid office matches your child's name with the Student Aid Report they received, because their college name appeared on the FAFSA application. FAFSA will send Student Aid Reports to ten colleges without charge. The Financial Aid Office reviews the Student Aid Report and puts together a financial aid package based on academic scores and the amount of financial need they can meet. Yup. That was not a misquote. Very few schools fund 100 percent of financial need.

On the bright side, the federal government no longer sends the names of colleges listed on the application to the other schools, which had allowed the Admissions Office to see whether they were your first or last choice.

In addition to federal aid, colleges and universities set aside their own academic scholarship funds for students who landed in the "Grab-This-One-Quick" basket. How does a student get there? Look inside the basket, which contains students with GPA and SAT scores in the upper 25 percent of the incoming freshman class. So, the first trick to increasing financial aid is to apply to a college where your son's or daughter's scores are within that top 25 percent bracket. This information is available in college guidebooks and online.

For the record, there are three options for attending 2- and 4-year higher-education programs:
1. Public colleges and universities
2. Private non-profit colleges and universities
3. For-profit schools and online universities.
   If you are considering this option, read chapter fifteen.

The Student Aid Report (SAR)
The Student Aid Report, based on your FAFSA application, gives you a bottom-line number called the Expected Family Contribution (**EFC**) which is the amount of money the government believes you can afford to pay for college. Whether you can or can't never enters the computer's mind. Everyone's EFC is calculated with the same federal formula called the Federal Method or FM. This is how it works:

If my Expected Family Contribution is $30,000 per year and College XYZ, the one my daughter selected, costs $65,000, we should receive $35,000 in financial aid to make up the difference. If my daughter attends college ABC, the one my wife and I thought would be a good idea, costing $25,000, we will receive no financial aid because our Expected Family Contribution is still $30,000. But paying $25,000 for college ABC is $5,000 cheaper than paying $30,000 for college XYZ. Of course, the fact that you will not receive the full amount of demonstrated financial need, forcing you to borrow money, is another story.

College Visit Checklist

While your son or daughter is ogling the new sports complex, salivating over the cafeteria's food choices and selecting a dormitory, find someone representing the Financial Aid Office and ask:

> 1. What percent of Demonstrated Financial Need do they meet?
> 2. What is the average freshman financial aid package?
> 3. What percentage of students graduate in four years?
> 4. What percentage of the faculty are part-time?
> 5. How does the college keep the cost of textbooks low?
> 6. Where can I find one of those cool school hats?

Schools are required to post retention rates, on-time graduation rates, and average indebtedness on their website. Good luck finding it. Assign that look-up to your college-bound and ask for a report before they leave the house to hang out with their friends to do whatever they do that you don't want to know about.

My wife and I always found campus visits informative and a lot of fun. As parents, we are on the lookout for student and instructor body language. Mannerisms reveal a lot about the school's atmosphere. We look at the campus buildings and grounds (do they have a blue-light safety system?) and wonder whether our daughter would enjoy living there for the next four years. We drive around the town or city surrounding the campus checking to see if it is a safe, crime-free area.

When should you begin visiting colleges? Start early, even in grade nine or ten. Consider it window shopping. Later on, you can sign up for a college tour. My daughter took her first college tour in grade ten, and by the way, that is the college she is attending today.

Warning. Many students do not get into their backup school because they didn't bother to visit, or interview and schools keep track of that.

Golden Rule

How do you select a college? Choose one or more in which your son's or daughter's GPA and SAT scores fit within the top 25 percent of the incoming freshman class. This will help ensure their acceptance and scholarship funding.

Of course the above does not include those hoity-toity Ivies with applicant pools greater than the population of Boston. Yes. Yes. I know. The American way is to reach for the stars and get into the best colleges America has to offer. But the fact is, 99% of the CEOs in every major corporation, along with every other great leader in our country did not, I repeat, did not graduate from a hoity-toity. Nothing personal.

The next section of the book is for your son or daughter to read and is our gift to you, so you don't have to play the heavy. We've included everything they'll eventually get around to doing (unless you do it for them) before submitting their college application. You're welcome.

Message for Students

This book is really for you, the college-bound student, because you get to go to school while your parents get to stay home and pay the bills, you know, like they've been doing for, since you were born. I'm a parent with a daughter who is now in college, so I speak for myself and every other parent when I say, if you are serious about attending college, you have five opportunities to achieve greatness, beginning with your sophomore year. Are you ready?

College Planning

Decide what you would like to study in college, or conversely, decide you can't decide. At least you've decided. It is okay to enter college as an undeclared major. Don't let anyone give you a hard time about that choice. When I went to college, most students couldn't tell you what they wanted to do, unless they were following in the footsteps of a family member, and no one declared a major until their sophomore year. The good courses weren't offered until then anyway. Today, colleges and universities allow you to check "undecided" under the major selection. Some even have counselors to help students explore options. Don't worry if you don't know. Acknowledging that you don't know is a valuable trait, one that is curiously missing in so many of our politicians and public commentators today.

On the other hand, if you know what you want to study in college, that's also great, but in fact, most students change their minds at least once before graduation, so keep your eyes open for alternative paths to glory; they are limitless and expanding faster than the universe. Take every opportunity to discuss your area of interest with others. The more feedback the better.

Your guidance counselor should provide you with college planning and ideas, and some states provide free college planning assistance. Using Google, type in the state and "higher education assistance authority" to find the resource nearest you. Some will be called agencies, others are called corporations, but they all carry out the same role. A list and links can be found on our website: www.survivingthecostogcollege.com.

College Visits

Before you visit a college, check them out online. Using Google, type the name of the college and the words "student review." You may find a large selection of conflicting and sometimes scary student information. These are fun to use as an icebreaker with your college tour guide. At the very least, though, ask:

---

1. What is the size of the freshman class?
2. How many students are in my major?
3. Where can I study when the dorm gets noisy?
4. What do students in my major do after graduation?

After the campus tour, hunt down some students. Ask them what they like about the school, the drawbacks, and their knowledge of your major. If you are impressed with the school, send an email to the department head or admissions and ask if they schedule an open house or if there is some other way for you to meet with an instructor or grad student. We attended a department event with professors and grad students that was so interesting my daughter put that college on the top of her list.

Back to your search engine. You can type in a college name and the words "student evaluation." Some colleges will post the student's rating of individual instructors. Most are terrific, but some are not. A few of them prefer conducting research and working with graduate students to teaching undergraduate classes. A few find undergraduate students tiresome. But in their defense, some freshmen are tiresome, some are even obnoxious, and 10 to 25 percent don't return anyway, giving professors reason to shake their collective heads.

Scholastic Aptitude Test

Da, da, da dum. Adults worry about their credit scores; students worry about their **SAT** scores. Of course, you know the importance of receiving the highest possible scores in the two areas of Reading and Math. The writing section is gone, along with having points taken off for wrong answers.

These scores will not only get you into college, they are used to decide if you are in the top 25 percent of the incoming freshman class, making you eligible for the Get-This-One-Quick box and a sizable merit-based scholarship. Your high scores make you and the college look good. An alternate test is the **American College Test** (**ACT**). Your guidance department knows which test is preferred. Many colleges and universities are becoming SAT-optional, recognizing that four years of high school grades mean more than four hours of sitting in a chair taking a test.

With an SAT-optional school, however, you must have good grades, write a sparkling essay, and do very well in an interview if you request one. This is more in line with your future world of work. Some people might say the "real world," but college is your real world and you have every right to be proud of your hard work and effort.

Warning. Want to know how the National Leadership Conference and other student event organizers know how smart you are and invite you to attend one of their very expensive national conferences? The folks at SAT and ACT sell your personal information to marketers. Just thought you'd like to know. you already know about Facebook and Snapchat, Right? The second **Issue** is that these conference leaders would have you believe that attending their conference and putting that information on your college resume will increase your chances of being accepted. There is no evidence to support that claim.

College Essay

Your student essay will be read by a college admissions officer to help decide who you are and how well you write. Several websites offer essay writing suggestions. Two of my favorites are MIT Admissions and US News Education. Google "college essay" and take your pick. Harvard groups their essays into seven categories: Identity, Introspection, Overcoming Obstacles, Foreign Life, Passion, Inspiration, and Experience. If you have a clever or cute idea to grab the reader's attention, forget it. Apply the KISS principle. Keep It Simple Stupid. The best way to learn how to write a good essay is to read good essays written by students who got in. The Harvard Crimson also publishes "50 Successful Harvard Application Essays." The essays are a joy to read. Get the book and read it for fun. After writing your first draft, put it away. A week later edit out the adverbs, passive voices and the words "that," "which," and "it." Ask your favorite English teacher to read your essay and make suggestions. After all that, the serious rewriting begins. One of my daughter's friends wrote one of the most beautiful essays I've ever read. How did she do it? She put everything aside and wrote from her heart.

Don't Screw Up in Your Senior Year

After you've been accepted into college, don't slack off during the last half of your senior year. Don't fail a subject in your final semester. Don't break the law. Don't get arrested. Don't post uncomplimentary pictures on social media and don't make unflattering remarks about anyone or anything anywhere at any time. Bide your time and bite your tongue. Why? Because on more than one occasion, these failures of judgment have gotten back to the college and they withdrew their acceptance letter. Got the message?

And Now for Some Things Completely Different

The three most important **numbers** in your college admission file are GPA, SAT, and EFC. You know about GPAs and SATs, but what about the EFC? If you're not sure, read the parent section when they're not around. You'll learn FAFSA produces a Student Aid Report (SAR) containing a magic number called an EFC (Expected Family Contribution). This is the amount of money the government calculates your parents can afford to pay for you to go to college.

Why do the colleges want the EFC? Because in your quest for merit-based scholarships, the school will figure out how much federal aid they can include in your financial aid package. Why? Because they want to use government money before they use their own, the same way you want to spend your parent's money before you open your wallet. And of course, your parents want to receive as much private and federal money as possible before they spend their money.

The Common Application

More than five hundred schools accept the Common Application which you can find online at "www.commonapp.org." This makes the process too easy to send applications off to a lot of schools. More than one admissions officer has complained about having to wade through applications from students who are not serious, are reaching for the unobtainable, or casting a wide net hoping for the best. This also makes it too easy to spend a lot of money as each application costs $50.00 or more. Ten applications is $500.00. On the flip side, a very nice feature of the common app website is you can type in a school name and find their application deadlines, application fees, and their number of required written recommendations.

Didn't get your first choice and still want to go? Take your second choice, work your tail off to get straight A's during your freshman year, then transfer into your first-choice school. Over a thousand students transfer every year. No biggie.

Get Organized

Start your folder system early and keep all your junk together. Keep your folders in <u>ONE</u> place and keep on top of your application process. Don't trust that overworked guidance counselors will get your transcripts in on time. Camp outside their door until transcripts and recommendations have been sent. They'll appreciate your company.

Good luck in school

Chapter Four

How Much Money is Available?

The federal government expects parents and their children to pay for college, unlike Canada and other countries around the world that offer free tuition to their students. In the meantime, FAFSA is designed to offset some of these college expenses for those unable to pay, not for those who prefer to pay less, which of course, is you, me, and everyone else.

There are two basic concepts to keep in mind.
1. The amount of <u>government</u> <u>financial aid</u> you receive is based on your income. The less money you earn the more you receive.
2. The amount of <u>scholarship money</u> you receive is based on your GPA and SAT scores. The higher the score the more money you receive.

Attaining a <u>college education</u> and <u>home ownership</u> are two legs of the "American Dream." Both are extremely expensive, but the cost of college has the greatest impact because the burden, often costing as much as a house, is paid for over four years (not counting loans), whereas a home mortgage is spread out over thirty years. The third leg of the "American Dream" is a <u>good job</u> to pay for the first two legs. I hope this will be true for your children and true for mine. A million kids up to their ears in debt with no sign of a good job have not been so lucky.

> The federal government provides 167 billion
> dollars in higher education student aid, sort of.
> > Federal Grants 30 billion
> > Federal Work-Study Grants 1 billion
> > Student Loans 99 billion
> > Tax Benefits 36 billion
> In addition, students have access to state,
> college, and private scholarships.

Federal Grants, 30 Billion Dollars

Pell Grants

Pell Grants are the largest higher education federal grant program providing federal aid to 8 million undergraduate students in financial need. The maximum award is $6,095 each year beginning 2018. Pell Grants do not have to be paid back.

Supplemental Education Opportunities Grant program (SEOG)

The **SEOG** program is administered by the college, which also contributes 1/3 of the allocation. Thus, for every three dollars of federal allocation, the college adds one more. These grants are for financial need students, providing up to $4,000 each year and do not have to be paid back.

Teacher Education Assistance for College and Higher Education

The TEACH program offers grants for undergraduate students who are willing to teach in designated teacher shortage areas for four years. The maximum grant is $4,000 each year and does not have to be paid back

Iraq and Afghanistan Service Grant

This grant is for students whose parent or guardian died as a result of military service in Iraq or Afghanistan. The maximum grant award is the same as the Pell Grant and does not have to be paid back.

Work-Study Grants, 1 Billion Dollars

The Federal Work-Study program provides colleges with 75 percent of the money they use to pay students for part-time work. This is a good deal for students and a good deal for the school. Eligibility is based on need. Students may work up to 20 hours or less per week but never more than 8 hours per day. This money does not have to be paid back and is not counted as earned income by FAFSA. There is no better deal in town.

Federal Loans, 99 Billion

The federal student loan program is available to all students. Some loans are based on financial need, others are not. All loans, except Perkins Loans, are provided through the Direct Loan program and issued by the Department of Education through the college finance office.

Direct Loans come in two flavors

1. Subsidized loans for undergraduates with financial need as determined by FAFSA can be up to $3,500 for freshmen students, $4,500 for sophomores and $5,500 for juniors and seniors. Interest rate was 4.45 percent in 2018, plus a 1% origination fee which is deducted from your monthly payment. The interest due on these loans is subsidized the government while the student is in college at least half time. Students are not charged interest until six months after they graduate.

2. Unsubsidized loans for undergraduates with financial need as determined by FAFSA can be up to $5,500 for freshmen students, $6,500 for sophomores and $7,500 for juniors and seniors. These loans accrue interest from the date the funds are dispersed. If you do not pay this interest while in college, the original $5,500 loan becomes a $6,479 loan, an 18% increase. And don't forget to add a 1% origination fee on top of that. Multiply those numbers by four if you borrow money each year until graduation.

Perkins Loans

New funding for a **Perkins Loan** was discontinued by the feds as of 2018-2019 school year. Students holding a Perkins loan are still responsible for paying back these loans but no additional money is available.

Parent Loan for Undergraduate Students (PLUS)

PLUS loans are taken out by parents of undergraduate students for as much money as is required to pay for college costs not covered by the financial aid package. Graduate students may also borrow money from this program. You pay an origination fee of 4.264 percent and an interest rate of 7 percent and it is only a good deal for the financial institutions fronting the money. If you own a home, compare the rate with a home equity line of credit (HELOC) instead, which is based on prime plus a percentage. My bank's line of credit rate is 4 1/2 percent at this writing.

You do not need to become an expert in the various federal aid programs, because the financial aid office will let you know what they have to offer to your son or daughter.

Student Debt: The dark side of student loans

The average national student loan debt for public colleges is $35,500, depending on your information source. For private non-profit colleges, the debt is $32,300, and for private for-profit schools it's $39,950. Let me bring this closer to home. If a student borrows $5,500 a year to attend college, a small amount by most standards, it will add up to $22,000 in four years. With a ten-year federal Direct Loan at 4.45 percent (plus an origination fee of 1.069), monthly payments would be $227.47 which includes paying $7,296 in interest. If you had been able to save that $22,000 over a ten or fifteen-year period, you would have automatically saved another $7,296 by not having to borrow the money. That amounts to forty percent bonus award for being frugal with your money in the first place.

But the bigger problem is, these federal loans are often not enough to pay for college, requiring parents to take a second or third more expensive loan. Here are two examples of what could happen:

A. If, after graduation, the student cannot find the job they were hoping for and ends up earning $10.00 an hour for a forty-hour week, their monthly gross pay would be $1,600 reduced by federal and state taxes to about $1,200 and reduced again to $973 by the student loan payment of $227. This places the student's disposable income below the United States poverty threshold of $980.83 a month for a single person and is one reason 650,000 students (nearly half of them attended for-profit colleges) have defaulted on their student loans.[5]

B. If a student earned $17.00 an hour or an annual salary of $35,360, their monthly gross income would be $2,720 with $1,790 left over after taxes and making their loan payment. $35,360 represents the approximate beginning pay for **teachers**, **police officers,** and **firefighters** in the United States. $1,790 is barely enough to pay for housing, food, and transportation, raise a family, and save for a down payment on a house. Ironically, after four or more years of college, the beginning salary of these professionals is less than $49,900, making them eligible under the Simplified Needs Test for federal aid that may not have been available to them while living with their parents, which is why one parent noted wryly the cheapest way to send his daughter to college would be to marry her off.

The Institute for College Access and Success provides a wealth of current debt information, including the average student debt for every college in the country. Either Google or go to "www.ticas.org." Simply put, if there were enough jobs available in the major fields offered by colleges, the students would be able to pay their debt, but jobs are lacking even for students majoring in science, technology, engineering and math. I spoke with the parents of a college graduate in New Hampshire. He was looking for a job, two years after completing his degree in electrical engineering. The unemployment rate of people ages 18 to 24 hovers around 9 percent and many of those are college graduates, or college drop-outs who could no longer afford to borrow the money they needed to finish their degree.

State Financial Aid

Millions of dollars are available in state aid with each state managing its own funds. Go to our website and then to Financial Resources. Click "State Grants." Select your state and go to their website. Student loans provided by the state are often less expensive then federal loans, but do not carry the federal protection of loan forgiveness or federal repayment plans. Each state divides financial aid into categories, reflecting their higher education programs and priorities. Many states provide counselors to answer your questions.

Private Financial Aid

Institutional Scholarships

Schools will use the terms scholarships and grants interchangeably. I prefer "scholarships" because they make you look smarter, except for the athletic kind. Only kidding! This is not federal money. The money comes out of the school's endowment funds, and they decide how it will be spent. Some scholarships are based on student need, but many are based on the school's need to bring in a certain type and level of student to ensure the continuance of quality programs. Good schools need good students. These funds are merit based in certain academic fields, fine arts, or athletics. The amount of scholarship ranges from a few thousand dollars to full tuition.

If your college-bound student is accepted into a private college and lands in the get-this-one-quick basket, they may receive a full ride. Harvard, Yale, and Princeton are famous for this, but when endowment funds exceed 32 billion, 20 billion, and 18 billion dollars respectively, offering a full scholarship is little more than a faculty Christmas party and a few flights to Bermuda. Stanford University recently announced that any student in a family with an AGI of $125,000 or less will receive a scholarship that will cover tuition, room and board. Brown University also has a reputation for giving students a free ride. College grants and scholarships do not have to be paid back, and the dollar value is not reported on your income tax return (yet). The scholarships are, in fact, a discount on the cost of attending that school.

One-of-a-Kind Scholarships
Grants and scholarships. You can search the internet for scholarships using a search engine and do not need to pay for this service. The college financial aid office is aware of many of these and may match you up. So, if you are six feet tall and would like a thousand-dollar scholarship, contact the closest "Tall Club" near you. If you live in Massachusetts, the local chapter is called the "Boston Beanstalks Tall Club." Seriously.

Private Scholarships
Private scholarships are available from religious organizations, service organizations, unions, banks, insurance companies, and large corporations. Your high school guidance office should have this information. We know one high school guidance office that emails every senior a list of scholarships listed in their files. Keep an eye on your local newspaper in the spring for pictures of the donating organization and winning recipients. You can also search online. These companies and agencies give money away for the publicity and tax benefit they receive, so you should be able to find them.

Remember this, however: Scholarship money must be reported on your annual FAFSA application and may be deducted from your next financial aid package, though receiving a scholarship you do not pay back is better than a loan you must pay back.

Corporate Scholarships
Think Coca-Cola, Gates Foundation, John F. Kennedy Profile in Courage Essay Scholarship, Buick Scholarships for car design, Siemens Scholarship, Apple Scholarships (which requires creating an app), Intel Scholarships, and even Colonel Sanders has some money to spread around.

Important. All of this information is online. You do not have to ask anyone to find this information for you. Begin with our website for the ones we found worked for us.

Post 9/11 GI Bill Transfer of Education Benefits
While President Franklin Roosevelt geared America's industrial production to support our troops plus those of England and Russia to combat the Axis during World War II, his wife Eleanor badgered him into preparing the country for the return home of our "boys." Thus was born the GI Bill of Rights to help pay for college and provide low-interest rates for home buyers. More homes and colleges were built right after the war than at any other time. Today, through the Post 9/11 GI Bill with a Transfer of Educational Benefits (**TEB)**, spouses and dependent children have access to the service members' unused benefits, which includes money to pay for college. Transferors use the Transfer of Education Benefits website to designate, modify, and revoke a Transfer of Entitlement (**TOE**) request. Eligibility is open to any member of the armed forces who has been in active duty and/or Selected Reserve with six years of service on the date of approval and who agree to serve four additional years from the date of election. Students taking advantage of this bill attend public colleges and universities, which agree to offset up to 50 percent of costs. The Department of Veterans Affairs matches the same amount. In 2009, the Yellow Ribbon program began funding private school tuition amounts exceeding the public in-state tuition rate. Veterans should not overlook these valuable benefits.

Chapter Five

Rules of the Game

Early Warning System

Parents need to know how much the government expects them to pay for college, or conversely, what they might expect to receive in financial aid, which is the difference between the Cost of Attending (COA) and their EFC. The sooner you know, the more time you will have to prepare for the financial onslaught. Three days' notice to board up your house threatened by a hurricane is better than having no time at all, which happened in 1939 along the North Atlantic coast, costing hundreds of lives. Or two hours' notice to duck into your basement at the threat of a tornado is better than looking out the rearview mirror of your car at a swirling mass of debris running up behind you. How much time to do you need to prepare? When should the early warning system sirens fire up on your behalf?

In the worst-case scenario of finding out what the government expects you to pay for your son or daughter to roam the ivy halls and hang out on the quad, the swirling debris is already kicking at your front door. Unfortunately, the worst-case scenario is the most common scenario for parents who don't prepare until their college-bound student is a senior sleeping late Saturday morning instead of filling out a college application.

The Free Application for Federal Student Aid (FAFSA) comes online in October, allowing you to fill it out with estimated 1040 tax numbers from the previous year. Colleges use the EFC to determine student aid eligibility, but don't send an offer of financial assistance until February or March. This gives you four months to scramble for six to twenty-six thousand dollars to pay at least half a year of tuition, room, board, books, and fees, depending upon the school's cost. When would you like the early warning system to kick in? How much time do you need to prepare? Six months? A Year? Five years?

Today we have early warning systems in place for hurricanes, tornados, tsunamis, floods (the very first was Noah building an ark), incoming missiles, epidemics, pollen count, heat waves, and events on your smart phone's calendar, but there is no early warning system for the amount of money you will be expected to pay for college. None. It is up to you, just as it was for those British subjects living in Concord and Lexington to figure out how to warn their neighbors in 1775 that the British were coming.

To create your own early warning system years in advance, use the EFC Formula on our website to calculate your Expected Family Contribution. If you find that your EFC is $21,000 and your son or daughter is in the 5th grade, you have seven years to prepare. If you calculate your EFC for the first time when your son or daughter is a senior, then most likely there is a swirling mass of debris running up against your rear bumper. The earlier you begin to plan, preferably when your son or daughter is in kindergarten, the better chance you will have of surviving the strong winds ahead.

Risk Management

No matter where you are in time, you must take on the role of Risk Manager for the future of your children. You must identify, review, control, and evaluate every aspect related to financing their college education. Don't leave it to the whims of others or the advice of friends and in-laws. Dig in and do it yourself. Become awesome! The first step of a risk manager is learning your EFC and understanding how to take advantage of the federal formula used to calculate your share of sending your child to college.

Analyzing the Federal Formula

You can't win the game unless you know the rules and use them to your advantage. The four parts to the federal formula should be thought of as four separate expected family contributions. As you review each section, think of the glass labeled EFC (Expected Family Contribution.) This glass will hold the amount of money you're expected to pay for college. Let's hope we can keep it half empty.

1. Students' Income reported to the IRS is protected in the federal formula up to $6,570 (2018). Any amount earned over that number is dumped into the EFC glass, becoming part of the total. Because federal and Social Security taxes are deducted, students can earn a little more and be safe. If the student earns $8,000, however, about $1,600 is added to the EFC glass. Does anyone have a high school teenager earning more than that amount of money? Not many. So, this threshold number may not become important until the student is attending college and working part-time to pay the bills. Are there ways around this? Of course.

2. Student assets are not protected at all. Twenty percent of a student's savings, CDs, etc. are also dumped into the EFC glass. You can prevent this from happening by putting the assets into the parents' name. NOTE: Private colleges using the CSS/Profile ask for tax information from two years back, which means this strategy would have to be employed before that time period. How does the financial office know? They see the interest earned reported on your tax return.

3. Parent income is assessed by a federal formula written into federal law. Like your income tax, you fill in the form and a computer spits out a number. In this case, the number gets dumped into the EFC glass as part of the amount you are expected to pay for college. This number is the "deductible." Until you reach it, the feds won't kick in a dime. The only way to reduce the EFC is to reduce your income, and you don't want to do that. And by the way, whether you spend all your money to pay bills or only half and put the rest in your pocket, makes no difference. The federal formula doesn't care how much you owe or have to spend to keep your head above water, or how much you get to keep, so stop crying.

How old will you be when your child goes to college? Find that age on the income protection allowance chart (table A3) and memorize the deductible. In the Federal Method (FM) formula, you get to subtract that income protection amount, along with a state tax allowance, Social Security tax allowance, income tax paid allowance, and an employment expense allowance from your adjusted gross income. The EFC amount is calculated from that adjusted income figure.

4. **Parent Assets** (savings, CDs, stocks, secondary property) are assessed at 5.64 percent after you deduct the Savings Protection Allowance. Your protected amount is based on your age; the older you are, the more you get to keep. Your protected amount should be lodged in your pre-frontal cortex for immediate retrieval along with your Social Security number, your spouse's birthday, and your anniversary date.

> Rule of thumb: Every asset in the parent's and student's name stays on the table unless it is in legal dispute, or subject to a lien. The four exceptions are: the house you live in, your retirement, life insurance, and personal items including cars, boats, paintings, and antiques.

How are we doing with the EFC glass? The glass should not contain an EFC contribution from student income or student assets and zero or minimal EFC contribution from parent assets. The EFC glass should only contain the EFC dollars based on the parent's income. Let's take a closer look at this by moving on to a financial package based on demonstrated financial need.

Demonstrated Financial Need

All we really want to know is, "How much do we get?" and, of course, the answer depends on the cost of the school. The government only kicks in after you have met your "EFC deductible," which is why we borrow millions of dollars every year to get educated. And boy, do we get an education. The formula for coming up with our Demonstrated Financial Need is the Cost of Attending college minus our Expected Family Contribution or (COA-EFC=DFN).

Here is an expanded example discussed in "Message to Parents" under Student Aid Report. If your expected family contribution is $25,000 and the private college costs $60,000, the demonstrated financial need is $35,000 (60,000 - 25,000). The financial aid package in grants, loans, and work-study should be $35,000, enough to pay the bills. The reality is otherwise, but we're not here to quibble, are we?

However, if your state college costs $25,000, the demonstrated financial need is $0.00 because your deductible of $25,000 is enough to pay the bills with one important exception. If you have two students in college at the same time, each costing $25,000 (or $50,000 total), your EFC now becomes $25,000 divided by two, or $12,500 per student. Feel better? More about this under "Double Benefit" later in the book on page 63.

The Gap or Unmet Need

The bad news. Very few schools fund 100 percent of Demonstrated Financial Need, creating a gap between the financial aid package and the money necessary to pay the cost of college. The U.S. News Education Edition survey of colleges and universities found only 62 (6 percent) of the 1,137 institutions that responded said they met 100 percent of the students' Demonstrated Financial Need. So, while the EFC on paper is $25,000, the actual cost could jump to $30,000 or more, requiring a loan of $5,000 to fill the gap.

The Daughter of John and Mary Smith

When John and Mary Smith's daughter entered the tenth grade, they knew she was headed for college and wanted to be ready for that expense when the time came. They pulled all their bank statements, income tax returns and W2s, and filled out the EFC/FAFSA Data Collection Sheet shown below. Now they had collected on one sheet all the information they would need to calculate their Expected Family Contribution number three years in advance.

John and Mary Smith EFC Data Sheet

P. #	Student Demographics	
	Student Social Security Number	036-72-1111
	Student driver's license number	RI 456789
	Are you interested in work-study	Answer "Yes"
	Parent 1 highest school grade completed	College
	Parent 2 Highest school grade completed	College
	College Selection: list names, addresses and Federal Codes on back	
	Parent Demographic Information	
	Month and year parents were married	09-1995
	Parent 1 Social Security number	036-38-4444
	Parent 1 date of birth	01-01-1972
	Parent 2 Social Security number	036-67-5555
	Parent 2 date of birth	07-06-1973
	Parent's email address	Happydaze33@
	Number of people in household	4
	Number of people attending college	1

	Parent Income Tax Information	
	Select "have filed" or "will file."	has filed
	Tax filing status (single, jointly, etc.)	Married jointly
	Type of income tax return. (1040, 1040A or 1040EZ	1040
1	Parents' adjusted gross income 1040-line 37	95,000
2a	Parent 1 Income earned from work	65,000
2b	Parent 2 Income earned from work	30,000
8	U.S. income tax paid 1040-lines 55-46	9,720
	Number of claimed exemptions 1040-line 6d	4
6	Additional information FAFSA #93a - 93f	0
4	Total untaxed income FAFSA lines #94a - 94i	0
16	Cash, checking, savings	11,000
17	Net worth of investments	0
18	Net worth of business	0
	Student Income Tax Information	
29	Adjusted Gross Income	3,500
30	Income earned from work salaries, tips, etc.	3,500
34	Additional information FAFSA #44a - 44f	0
32	Untaxed income and benefits FAFSA #45a - 45j	0
36	U.S. income tax paid	0
45	Cash, savings, and checking	6,000
46	Net worth of investments, stocks, bonds, trusts	0
47	Net worth of business	0

John and Mary used their worksheet to fill out the Federal EFC Formula to calculate their Expected Family Contribution

EFC FORMULA A: DEPENDENT STUDENT 2018-2019

PARENTS' INCOME				AVAILABLE INCOME	
1. Parents' Adjusted Gross Income	95,000			Total income from line 7	95,000
2a. Parent 1 income **$65,000**				Subtract Total allowances from line 14	53,908
2b. Parent 2 income **$30,000**				15. **AVAILABLE INCOME**	41,092
Total of parent #1 & #2 income	95,000				
3. Parents' Taxable income Tax filers enter from line 1 Non-tax filers enter line 2	95,000			**PARENTS CONTRIBUTION FROM ASSETS**	
4. Total untaxed income and benefits FAFSA question #94	0			16. Cash savings and checking	11,000
5. Total income (L3/4)	95,000			17. Net worth of investments	0
6. Total additional financial information FAFSA question #93.	0			18. Net worth of business or	
7. **Total Income**. Line 5 - line 6.	95,000			19. Adjusted net worth of business/ farm **TABLE A4**	0
				20. **Net Worth**. Sum lines 16,17 & 19	11,000
ALLOWANCES AGAINST PARENT'S INCOME				21. education savings and assets Use **TABLE A5**	19,800
8. Federal income tax paid	9,720			22. Discretionary net worth L20 - L21	0
9. Tax allowance. **TABLE A 1** +	4,750			23. Asset conversion rate	.12
10. Parent 1 social security **TABLE A2**	4,973			**24. CONTRIBUTION FROM ASSETS**	0
11. Parent 2 social security **TABLE A2**	2,295				
12. Income protection **TABLE A3**	28,170			**PARENTS' CONTRIBUTION**	
13. Employment expense Allowance:				**AVAILABLE INCOME** from line 15	41,092
				CONTRIBUTION **FOR ASSETS from** line 24	0
				25. Adjusted Available Income (AAI)	41,092
				26. Total parents' contribution AAI Calculate using **TABLE A6**	12,715
				27. Number in college	1
	4,000			28.**PARENTS' CONTRIBUTION** Divide by number in line 27	12,715
14. **TOTAL ALLOWANCES** 8 through 13 =	53,908				

Line 26 formula: $8,959 + 47\%$ of AAI over $33,100. = $12,715.24

STUDENT INCOME				STUDENT'S CONTRIBUTION	
29. Adjusted Gross Income	3,500			45. Cash, savings & checking	6,000
30. Income earned from work	3,500			46. Net worth of investments	0
31. Taxable income Tax filers enter amount from line 29 Non-tax filers enter from line 30	3,500			47. Net worth of business and/ or investment farm	0
32. Total untaxed income and benefits See FAFSA question # 45	0			48. **Net worth** Sum lines 45 - 47	6,000
33. Total taxable and untaxed income	3,500			49. Assessment rate	0.20
34. Total additional financial information FAFSA question # 44	0			50. STUDENT'S ASSETS CONTRIBUTION	1,200
35. TOTAL INCOME Line 33 minus line 34	3,500				
				EXPECTED FAMILY CONTRIBUTION	
ALLOWANCES AGAINST STUDENT INCOME				**PARENTS' CONTRIBUTION** from line 28	12,715
36. U.S. income tax paid last year	0			**STUDENT'S CONTRIBUTION FROM AI** from line 44	0
37. State allowance **TABLE A7**	105			**STUDENT'S CONTRIBUTION FROM ASSETS** from line 50	1,200
38. Social Security allow **TABLE A2**	0			**51. EXPECTED FAMILY CONTRIBUTION**	13,915
39. Income protection allowance	6,570				
40. Allowance for parents' negative Adjusted Available Income. If line 25 is negative, enter line 25 as a positive number. If line 25 is zero or positive, enter zero here.	0				
41. **TOTAL ALLOWANCES**	6,675				
STUDENT'S CONTRIBUTION FROM INCOME					
Total Income from line 35 above	3,500				
Total allowances from line 41 above	6,675				
42. **Available income (AI)**	0				
43. Assessment of AI	.50				
44. STUDENT'S CONTRIBUTION FROM AI =	0				

The EFC of $13,915 was reduced to $12,715 when Mr. Smith eliminated his daughter's saving account.

These forms are in the back of the book an on the website.

Chapter Six

Beating the Odds

Two Case Studies

John and Mary Smith. Their daughter, Mary Jr., is ready for college. Their FAFSA/EFC worksheet and EFC Formula sheet are printed in the previous chapter. They started a savings account, depositing $20.00 a week for 10 years. The account is now worth $11,000. Mary Jr. is a hard worker and will do well in life. She saved $6,000 of her earnings in an account under her name. John is a hands-on guy who likes to take things apart to see how they work. In his daughter's sophomore year, he printed out the federal government EFC Formula sheet to calculate his expected family contribution. He found he was responsible for paying $13,915 a year toward his daughter's college expenses. He also noticed line #23 assessed the family assets at 12 percent while line #49 assessed his daughter's assets at 20 percent. To see what difference it would make, he changed his daughter's assets to zero and added her $6,000 to his savings, bringing his total up to $17,000. What happened when he recalculated? Their original EFC of $13,915 was reduced to $12,715, a savings of $1,200 for each year of college or $4,800 over four years. When he thought about the savings, it made perfect sense. Twenty percent of $6,000 is $1,200 he no longer had to add to his Expected Family Contribution.

For the record, John, age 45, qualifies for $19,800 (2018) in asset protection based on his age. By combining the $11,000 with their daughter's $6,000 under their name, the total amount of $17,000 was fully protected. We said earlier, John's a hands-on guy and with all the forms and tables in front of him he began to understand the rules of the game. This transfer of savings was a quick fix but must be completed at least a year before filling out FAFSA. While completing the EFC formula, John also saw his adjusted gross income of $95,000 reduced by $53,908 in state tax, social security, and income protection allowance and an employment expense allowance because both he and his wife worked. These allowances decreased their assessed income down to $41,092. Next case.

Adam and Eve Montana are an older couple with two boys. Their adjusted gross income is $160,000, and over the years they saved $200,000 while their college-age son had $24,000 in savings received from various relatives. Adam had no interest in filling out the FAFSA application because he assumed they earned too much money. He did, however, complete the EFC formula to prove his point. His EFC came out to $46,926, about $14,000 less than the $60,000 price tag of the private school, Noah University, their son would like to attend. They met with their accountant, who knew how the federal formula worked because he had a son in college. You know the first step, right? Adam and Eve eliminated their son's savings and put it in their account.

This step alone reduced their EFC by $4,800. Next, based on the accountant's advice, they took $140,000 of savings to pay off the mortgage and another $4,000 to pay off their credit card debt. This left them with $80,000 in assets, of which $29,600 is protected, leaving them with a balance of $50,400 to be included in the EFC formula. Now their original EFC of $46,926 is down to $35,358. With the mortgage and credit card debt paid off, their disposable monthly income increased by $1,600 or $19,200 a year. If you subtract this new available income from their EFC of $35,358, the additional amount they need to pay for college is down to $16,158. They expect their son to receive scholarship aid worth at least $10,000 and they still have $75,488 left in savings.

The price tag for Noah University is now manageable and a great sigh of relief is heard across the land.

Personal Financial Plan

Your personal financial plan revolves around what you believe is best for you and your family and is restricted by your present and future earnings. Your plan is also restricted by the number of years you have <u>before</u> filling out FAFSA. More years equals more options, more time to think the plan through, and more time to make adjustments along the way. You may have heard the saying *Failure to plan is planning to fail.* Unfortunately, this is true.

When you are developing your own financial plan, remember the following assets <u>are on the table </u>and counted against you in the federal formula:
1. Parents' income minus protected allowance
2 Parents' assets minus protected allowance
3. Student income minus protected allowance. $6,570
4. Twenty percent of student savings
5. Second residence net value

The following assets are <u>off the table</u> and not counted against you.

1. Personal residence
2. Life insurance
3. Retirement savings
4. Personal possessions including cars, boats, etc.
5. Parents' income protection allowance
6. Parents' savings allowance
7. Assets owned by a person not living in home

Well, I hope this gives you some ideas. And since forewarned is forearmed, now would be a good time to find out what your EFC would be if your college-bound student received an acceptance from one of those very expensive schools.

Chapter Seven

EFC Formula and Net Price Calculator

You know that the Expected Family Contribution is a number calculated by the federal formula, which is subtracted from the cost of attending college. The remainder of that subtraction becomes your demonstrated financial need, and the basis for all need-based federal grants and loans.

The most accurate picture of what the government believes you can pay for college before you fill out FAFSA online is the completed EFC FORMULA worksheet used by John and Mary Smith in chapter six. You could skip it and wait to see what magic number Uncle Sam gives you after you fill out the FAFSA application, or you can peek into his books and learn ahead of time.

The purpose of filling out this form in advance, indeed the purpose of this entire book, is to help you understand the Federal Formula and to use that information to your advantage to create an individual financial plan to pay for college.

Your next step? Put the book down and go to the companion website

www.survivingthecostofcollege.com

Click on "Book Resources" and you will find these forms. Download the Data Collection form used in this book or select the Excel Four-Year spread sheet that you can download to your computer for use.

Then download the Federal Formula Guide that has forms for dependent and independent students and tables A1 through A7.

This may seem daunting at first, but once you fill in the Data Collection Sheet, which you will need to fill out FAFSA anyway, completing the EFC formula is easy.

Calculating Your EFC on the Internet

There are several internet sites that will calculate Expected Family Contribution. They are quick and easy to use but not always accurate. There are also sites that ask you to take surveys and ask for your personal information. You don't need to go there. Below are four internet sites I used to plug in Mary's information from chapter five and the results that came back:

Big Future College Board	EFC $14,869
TG Adventure in Education	EFC $12,706
FinAid	EFC $13,317
College Toolkit	EFC $14,394

Mary's final EFC was $12,175, making TG Adventure in Education the clear winner. I have no idea if that was a fluke, but after filling out the EFC Formula form, try them for yourself. The value of using the government's EFC Formula worksheet is learning how the formula works, giving you the information needed to create a financial plan to reduce your expected family contribution and survive the cost of college.

Net Price Calculator. The Internet Sticker Price

Beginning in 2011, colleges and universities were required to offer a net price calculator on their websites. The net price is the amount of money that comes out of your pocket to pay for college. They use current institutional statistics to provide an estimated net cost of college, which is the cost of attending minus grant and scholarship aid that does not have to be paid back. The key to receiving a significant award is the student's GPA and SAT scores.

The quickest way to find a school's net price calculator is to use a search engine. Type in the name of the school and the words "net price calculator." Trying to find it on the college's website could take a long time, especially if you are visiting for the first time.

The Net Price Calculator (NPC) is the quickest way to find a financial safety school by getting a rough estimate of how much merit-based scholarship money the school will offer your son or daughter in the best-case scenario.

1. GPA of 3.5 or better
2. Completed Honors and Advanced Placement classes
3. SAT score in the top 25% of incoming freshman

I used the net price calculator of one college, then called their finance office to ask how accurate my numbers were. I felt sorry for the young woman attempting to describe the vagaries of the system. Unfortunately, the NPC does not provide a definitive number and in the strictest sense, may not fulfill the original purpose of the legislation to help families learn whether the school is affordable, but it comes closer than anything else we have.

If a school's NPC tells you there is not enough merit-based money on the horizon, you might as well cross that school off your list. Remember Mary Smith from Rhode Island? Using the NPC, Mary's net price for attending the following schools are, at the time of this writing:

College	Cost to Go	Scholarship	Net price*
Rhode Island College	$20,776	$4,500	$16,276
U. of Rhode Island	$26,320	$6,500	$19,820
U. of New Hampshire	$45,459	$22,000	$23,459
University of Maine	$26,362	$16,490	$9,872

Tuition for the University of Maine is based on the New England Regional rate and the scholarship amount is a "Flagship Match." Each school is outstanding in its own way and Mary is fortunate to have so many good schools to choose from. And while students from all over the world come to New England for an education, a large number of teens wouldn't be caught dead attending a college in their own state for reasons known or not known only to them.

If you filled out the EFC Data Collection Sheet, you will have most of the required financial information to use the net price calculator. Additional information might include:

Student's GPA
SAT Scores
Parents' Earned Interest
Current value of your home
Purchase price of your home
Year home purchased
Out of pocket medical expenses
Student's interest earned

I simply wrote the information on the back of my daughter's data collection sheet, then completed the Net Price Calculator of a private college which asked more questions than most public institutions. Schools have the choice of using the bare minimum federal template with only a few questions for their calculator or developing a more comprehensive set of questions that will provide the student with a more accurate estimate. The private schools use the robust platform.

As I filled in the answers on each web page, I clicked my keyboard "Print Screen" and pasted the screen shot into a word document. This gave me a record of my answers to each question that I used later for comparisons. I then used the printout as a reference to fill out the calculator for additional schools. If this sounds like I don't have a life, you are right, at least while writing this book. Do I recommend you do all this work? Only if your family has left you.

As you can see from the NPC in Mary's case, each institution offers a different grant amount. There are many reasons for this but one you should not overlook is that institutions use scholarships to bolster various academic programs, e.g. nursing, engineering, and the arts. Schools also use scholarship money to increase diversity in target areas that are in line with their broader institutional goals. For example, Mary wants to become a Pediatric nurse, so she would be wise to search for a school that wants to expand their nursing program. Institutional goals, related to academics, are often backed up with additional student funding.

Important. If a website gives you the option of creating an account or signing on as a guest, <u>sign on as a guest</u> and when you complete the form, click "<u>do not save information</u>." This will assure that no one has your records for their personal use. At least that is what they say.

But what about Mary? Her EFC worksheet calculates an expected family contribution of $12,715. Why do colleges expect her to pay up to $24,772?

Well first, these are internet sticker prices for the purpose of helping you rule in or rule out a school's affordability. And second the school may offer additional scholarship money if you're in the "Grab-This-One-Quick basket. And third, unfortunately, much of the federal aid comes in the form of loans and these you have to pay back.

If Mary had applied to a private school, she would also have filled out the CSS/PROFILE to calculate an expected family contribution. The PROFILE application searches through your accounts two years back with a fine-tooth comb. They want to know the equity in your home, the value of your pre-tax retirement assets, and then they check your shed out back to see if you're spinning straw into gold.

However, the largess of private school scholarship money is based on the CSS profile calculations and, of course, the student's good grades and SAT scores. Millions of dollars are awarded every year to students by private colleges and universities to reduce or eliminate the cost of tuition. Several of the best schools in the country offer free tuition to students with family income below certain threshold levels.

In Mary's case, the Rhode Island, Maine and New Hampshire public institutions use the FAFSA calculated expected family contribution (EFC) number and fund the demonstrated need up to the amount their institution determines they can afford. Remember, only six percent of colleges in the United States reported funding 100 percent of the student's demonstrated need.

If Mary is willing to travel 300 miles north, the University of Maine looks like the best financial option. If she opts to remain in Rhode Island, Rhode Island College is the least expensive school for her to attend, though URI costs so little more, it would be worth comparing programs including graduation rates. We want Mary to finish in four years, not five or six.

In the end, the only number that matters is the one you read in your financial aid package; not how much you will receive, but the bottom line cost of college after the aid is deducted. Until then, all of life is an approximation. When it is over, parent responses range from "Why did we spend so much time worrying about this?" to "How are we going to afford this?" Hopefully your response will be the former.

Chapter eight

FAFSA-Land and the CSS PROFILE

The college application is one of two major forms college students fill out if they want to attend college. The other is the Free Application for Federal Student Aid (FAFSA). The first application gets you into college and the second helps you pay the bills. And although most parents fill out all or part of FAFSA, each of the hundred-plus questions are addressed to and can be filled out by the student.

The United States Department of Education provides close to 30 billion dollars in federal grants including Work-Study programs and 99 billion dollars for student loans. The college financial aid office determines which students are eligible for this money based on student and parent financial information reported in the Free Application for Federal Student Aid. The college also uses this information to help determine your eligibility for their grants and scholarships.

Using this information, a Federal Formula calculates and creates a single number called the Expected Family Contribution, or EFC. This is the amount of money the federal government believes you can afford to pay for college, and should college be more expensive, you may be eligible for grants, work-study, or loans to fill the gap. For example, after filling out FAFSA, you learn that your Expected Family Contribution (EFC) is $20,000. Your college-bound is accepted to a college or university that costs $35,000 for tuition, room and board, books, supplies, and transportation. The college could offer you a financial aid package of $15,000 to fill that gap in a combination of grants, work-study, and student loans.

It is important to remember that the Free Application for Federal Student Aid is free. There are online websites that charge a fee to help you fill out this form. Instead, go online to "fafsa.ed.gov".

FAFSA is not difficult to fill out and the financial information they request is nothing more than what you have reported on your 2016 tax return and the balance of your checking and savings accounts. If you own a business or a trust, that information is required as well. In the past, you could transfer your tax information to FAFSA using a Data Retrieval Tool, saving you the time of looking up this information, but the DRT has been shut down with no word from the Department of Education as to when it will reopen.

Filling out FAFSA does not have to be time-consuming or a burden if you organize your approach. After collecting my financial information, I filled out FAFSA online in about 30 minutes. You can do the same. FAFSA is organized into four major sections:

1. Student Demographics
2. Parent Demographics
3. Parent Financial Information
4. Student Financial Information

In addition to student demographics, you must list the colleges you want the Department of Education to send your report to.

Although you may not be eligible for a federal grant or work-study program based on your income, you will always be eligible for a federal PLUS loan. But, without an up-to-date FAFSA, the college financial aid office is unable to process a federal loan, leaving you to borrow money at higher rates of interest from a private financial institution.

When do you begin the process? FAFSA goes online October 1 and is used by the college financial aid office to disburse funds for the following school year. Once you fill out FAFSA, most of the information is transferred into the following year's application.

It is worth noting that the financial information they request and base their calculations (for 2018) comes from your 2016 income tax report. This creates a dilemma if your financial situation has changed since that time and becomes a legitimate reason to appeal your financial aid award. You can always send updated information to the college finance office or even appeal your financial package.

The disadvantage to filling out FAFSA in October or even November is that you may not have made your college selection. You can handle the problem this way. Type in the name of your state university and your application will be processed. Once you have made your final decision, reopen FAFSA and revise your college list.

Begin the process by collecting the information you will need to fill out FAFSA well before October 1, so you can finish the process by the end of October. Working on FAFSA during the holidays or after just adds stress to an already stressful time of year.

How do you get started? Students go online to register by creating a user name and password. Once you have begun filling out FAFSA, if you need a break or have a question, you can close the program and later return to where you left off.

When you have completed the application, print out your report, which is a paper version of your responses. At the bottom you will find your Expected Family Contribution (EFC) amount, which the federal formula has calculated. While FAFSA must be filled out for each year your child is in college to receive a grant or a loan, you only need to pull up last year's report and update the financial section.

If you have another child ready for college, you need to fill out one for each student. Though your financial information is the same, savings and assets of the second student are counted as part of the federal aid formula. However, the second application need not be that difficult to complete. Follow these steps.

Begin by revising the FAFSA of your student in college and print out the results. Next, using that printed information, fill out the new FAFSA for the second child. The only difference will be the student's information. And don't forget, your Expected Family Contribution now applies to two students, or is cut in half, making you eligible for additional financial aid for each student.

If your heart is racing or your anxiety has reached record highs, go to our website. Under Book Resources, you will be able to view and print out a PDF of the FAFSA, because I understand and appreciate that no amount of words here are as helpful and stress-reducing as seeing the document in front of you and finding out that it truly is a walk in the park.

FOUR STEPS TO SANITY   GET ORGANIZED.

1. Create a folder in your email account labeled College Admission into which you keep all emails sent and received related to college visits, admission, and everything else even remotely related to your college search, applications, and the submission of forms.

2. Set up a file folder for all the financial documents you will need to fill out FAFSA and the PROFILE application. Collect and add these documents and information no later than the first week in October. These include:

    a. Last federal income tax return
    b. W-2 forms, and records of untaxed income
    c. A list of bank accounts and their present balances
    d. Net value of stocks, bonds, trusts, and other investments
    e. Value of tax deferred and other retirement plans
    f. Untaxed social security benefits, flexible spending accounts for medical expense, 529 plans, retirement annuities, net value of home (estimate market value minus mortgage balance) grants and scholarships and student income.

g. A list of expenses, including child support, repayment of educational loans, out of pocket medical, dental and medication expenses, education tuition, and mortgage payments.

3. Go to our website www.survivingthecostofcollege.com and click on Print Forms. Download the FAFSA PDF application.

4. Register online (October 1) for FAFSA and the CSS PROFILE if required by your college. Print out the PROFILE worksheet and General Instruction sheet.

FILLING OUT THE FAFSA WORKSHEET

Fill out a blank **Data Collection Sheet,** the one used by the Smith family in the Rules of the Game chapter. Download this from the website under "Book Resources." If you are filling out only FAFSA you will have all the financial information you need. In either event, during the month of September fill out the FAFSA and profile worksheets in pencil at your leisure with a glass of wine or bottle of beer or whatever else increases your comfort level.

FILLING OUT FAFSA ONLINE

I have read that filling out the FAFSA application online can take between one and two hours. Most of that time is spent going back and forth between your computer and wherever you keep your bank records, tax information, and other financial information called for in the application. If you fill out the EFC/FAFSA Data Collection Sheet first, completing the application online shouldn't take more than 30 minutes. You can also fill out the paper version of FAFSA before going online to familiarize yourself with the questions, but the organization of the paper version is different from the online version and maddening to navigate. There is one value to printing out the paper version, however, and that is to review questions regarding untaxed income and benefits for the parent and the student, questions

94 and 45, and "Additional financial information" questions 93 and 44. The paper version is on our website.

Whether the parent fills out FAFSA or the student and parent fill out their sections separately, you can close the program down and return later. As we mentioned earlier in the book, you can have your son or daughter complete their sections, which includes the colleges they have selected, then close it down. The parents can fill in their information and send it out later. Of course, you can also do it all yourself.

Here are five tips to make answering FAFSA questions easier:

1. If you're not sure how to answer a questions requiring a number, enter zero.

2. When checking "yes" and "no" questions and you are not sure, check "no."

3. If your most recent tax information is not available because you haven't filed your income tax, it is okay to estimate these numbers based on the previous year's tax form because they revise your numbers later when you have completed your taxes. If you filled out the PROFILE, use the same numbers you reported in the "Parents' Expected Income and Benefits" section.

4. The most common mistake is leaving a question blank. Don't.

5. Be careful not to use a private website to fill out your application. These look like the government website but will cost you money after you have filled in your personal and financial information. Remember, FAFSA is FREE. Go online to "www.fafsa.ed.gov". Type in the student user name and password, then fill out the form using the worksheet as a reference, as early as October

but no later than the second week in January. Remember the whole process should only take thirty minutes.

As soon as you submit the application, you will receive a confirmation page. Print it out. The page lists the colleges you have selected and, most importantly, your estimated Expected Family Contribution amount in small print toward the bottom of the sheet under the category **Eligibility Information**. If you calculated your EFC earlier using the federal formula, the numbers should be the same. My numbers matched to the penny, even though the pennies are not included in the figures.

CSS PROFILE

If you are filling out the CSS PROFILE, begin with printing out the CSS Financial Aide PROFILE worksheet. Collect last year's tax records and this year's financial information, then gather up the courage to estimate what your1040 will look like at the end of this fiscal year, three months before it is over. You will need to scavenge up and list the net value of every asset in your name and the name of everyone in your family. October is the month to become an expert in your financial life. If you are slightly hazy on the details, they will become crystal clear during your research. If you do not do your taxes or spend time reviewing the completed forms and schedules prepared by someone else, now is the time to get acquainted. If you are not lined up at the starting gate on October 1 with a million other parents, you lose first consideration on the money available. If you do not organize early, the process becomes pure drudgery or worse. You do not want to be scurrying around your basement or attic looking for financial records during the Christmas holidays or in the dead of winter.

As we said, a college education begins with filling out the college application. Paying for that education begins with filling out the Free Application for Federal Student Aid (FAFSA), and for most private non-profit schools, filling out the CSS PROFILE is also required.

The CSS PROFILE becomes available October 1, the same date you can access FAFSA. The deadline for completing the CSS Profile is usually November 1 for early admission and February 1 for regular admission. Completing these applications online long before the deadline can be easy and reasonably stress-free if you follow these basic steps.

FILLING OUT THE CSS PROFILE

If you Google "CSS PROFILE" numerous websites pop up. To begin with, select the PDF version and print it out for your records. This will give a one-page overview of the program and a second page listing the 250+ schools that require the PROFILE.

CSS stands for "College Scholarship Services," the financial aid division of College Board, which administers the CSS Financial Aid Profile. They also administer the high school Advanced Placement (AP) exams, the PSAT and the SAT testing programs. Students will use their SAT identification code to log into College Board and will be familiar with this site. Go to "www.css.collegeboard.org" for an online interactive presentation to take you through the process, including how to submit the application and make payment. Yes, payment. This one isn't free.

Once you log into College Board, you can register to fill out the PROFILE. Registration includes selecting the colleges you want the PROFILE information sent to. After you register, click on and print out the Pre-Application Worksheet and General Instruction sheet.

DO NOT FILL OUT THE PROFILE ONLINE UNTIL YOU HAVE COMPLETED THE WORKSHEET AND FEEL COMFORTABLE WITH YOUR ANSWERS.

The PROFILE has eleven sections. The number and depth of those questions looks overwhelming but are easy to fill out if you have filled out the worksheet ahead of time. You may not appreciate the PROFILE's audit-like approach, but the results can open the door to millions of dollars in institutional financial aid, especially if your son or daughter is one those overachievers with off-the-grid GPAs and SAT scores. The eleven PROFILE sections are:

Parents' Data (PD). Asks for basic family information plus the value of any tax-deferred retirement plans. There will be a separate retirement question for each parent. You will have to decide who is parent #1 and parent #2. FAFSA asks the same question. Be consistent. Documents: Tax-deferred retirement plan statements.

Parents' Household Information (PH). Asks questions regarding food stamp and WIC benefits you may have received.

Parents' Most Recent Income and Benefits (PI). Asks questions about parents' income for the present year, the tax year in which your student is a senior in high school. If you are filling out the PROFILE in October, base your estimates on the first three quarters of your income. The worksheet will designate the tax year, so you won't go wrong. Each question includes the line on your income tax form 1040 from which to find or estimate the information. They will ask you to list untaxed social security benefits, flexible spending accounts for medical expenses, net income from your business, amount paid directly to tax-deferred pensions, and the value of veteran's non-educational benefits and work-study allowance. These are also the numbers you will use for filling out FAFSA. **The numbers should be the same on both forms!**

Parents' Previous Income and Benefits (PP). This section is a repeat of the one above but for the previous tax year when your student was a junior in high school. Questions include the line on your tax return from which to find the dollar amounts they are requesting. Now they have a two-year history of your finances.

Parents' Expected Income and Benefits for the Present Year (PF). This is the tax year in which your student will be a freshman in college. Estimate your numbers based on the numbers you reported in the PI section. This is the most important income reporting section because it shows the college financial aid office where you will be when your son or daughter is in college, not where you have been. Hopefully you had an opportunity to use some of the suggestions found in the book under Financial Planning to create a more favorable financial situation for filling out the PROFILE and FAFSA.

Parents' Assets (PA). Asks for the value of your assets as of the date you fill out the application. Assets include: cash, savings, checking, stocks and bonds, CDs, 529 plans, non-retirement annuities, assets held in the name of brothers and sisters, and the net value of your personal property (estimated market value minus mortgage debt) and other real estate. I would also subtract repairs that are needed on the property and real estate agent fees you would pay to sell the property from the net value. Your final number will be a good faith estimate which is acceptable.

Parents' Expenses (PE). While the PROFILE digs deep into your income and assets, it also provides you with an opportunity to list expenses. These include: child support, re-payment of educational loans, medical and dental expenses, education tuition for other children in the family, monthly mortgage payments and explanations of special circumstances.

Student Data (SD). This section asks you to list scholarships received in the previous year and the amount of money paid by the parents for the student's education. This question is a little tricky asking for estimates. A full explanation is available in the General Instructions PDF you printed out. Documents: tax records.

Student Present Income and Benefits (SI). Asks for the student's (and student's spouse if married) income, cash received, untaxed income, and benefits. Documents: tax records.

Student's Expected Income and Resources (SR). Asks about veteran's benefits, expected income in the coming year and the total amount of grants, scholarships, and fellowships the student has received or is expected to receive. They also want to know the amount the parents think they can pay, and the amount the student expects to receive from the parent's employer and from their relatives. Seriously, they really want a list of contributing relatives. Look out Uncle Joe and Aunt Mary, you're being reported.

Student's Assets (SA). Asks for a list of student assets including: savings, CDs, 529 plans, stocks, bonds, trusts, oil wells, and gold mines.

FILLING OUT THE CSS PROFILE ONLINE

Important: Before filling out the CSS PROFILE online, read all the instructions carefully. Pay attention to the process of saving, navigating, and printing/saving the program. Once you have registered and answered their preliminary questions, you are ready to go. Log back in if you are not already there. Your registration information will pop up, and you are ready to type in your worksheet answers. If you need a break, you can save your information, close the program down and return at any time. After you finish entering the data in October, you can sit back and enjoy a no-pressure Thanksgiving and Christmas. Happy Holidays.

BOOK REOURCES

FAFSA and CSS PROFILE applications and worksheets may be viewed and downloaded from our website. You will also find links to the government and College Board websites for registration. From our website click on "Applications."

Chapter Nine

Practical Solutions to Reducing Cost

College Funding Options

There are many ways to reduce the cost of college; the easiest is to attend a less expensive school. There are a hundred or more across the country. Google "Inexpensive Colleges" and compare lists. Read the "College Tuition on the Cheap." column on our website for more information. These practical solutions are organized in reverse order in the event you are reading this when your college-bound is a second semester senior and you've run out of options. The earlier you begin, the more options you will have. Financial planning for college begins at the birth of your child (like you have nothing else to do). So, we'll start with the last resort and work backward in time.

1. Appeal. When All Else Fails.

"It's not fair," you say. You may be right. Who am I to judge? If you cannot afford to send your son or daughter to college without additional federal or college aid and have unusual circumstances that you can document, e.g. high medical bills or caring for indigent parents, collect your documentation and your thoughts and prepare a non-threatening unemotional appeal. Most schools have the appeal process described and the Financial Aid Appeal form on their website that you can download and fill out. If not, when you are calm, pick up the phone and give the financial aid office a call. Request the name of the person who hears appeals. Talk to them on the phone and follow up with an email and copies of your documents if requested. If you do not live far away and have the time, request a meeting. They will be more than happy to hear what you have to say, especially if your son or daughter is in the top 20 percent of the incoming freshman class. The financial aid officer can adjust the input information to help you, but they cannot monkey with the formula. Many colleges and universities use an appeal committee to handle these requests. Go to our website and the Explore section. Read "Appealing a Financial Award" which includes a sample financial aid appeal form.

2. Commute to School

Living at home and commuting can cut your college bill almost in half. The only drawback is the limitation this plays in college selection, but if you have public transportation, an hour and a half ride is perfect for completing your assignments. We know students commuting to Brown University, Worcester Polytechnic Institute, and Bryant University. I drove an hour a day to Ohio State University for classes and thought nothing of it. Yes, you miss the "full college" experience, but at least you get to attend and without crushing debt, which ten years from now, will make a huge difference in your lifestyle. So, don't discount this option.

3. College Choice, A and B Schools

Rating colleges A and B is a method that allows parents to look at college selection within the framework of the student's educational goals and their own financial situation. If the educational goals can be reached with a bachelor's degree or less, the undergraduate college should have a good-to-excellent reputation in the student's major field. This includes technical schools, because my electrician, plumber, and auto mechanic earn more than I do. In this case, the schools become "A" colleges. An "A" college is the one you want to be in when you finish your education, but not necessarily when you begin your education. If your college-bound's goals require graduate school to become a professional in the field of accounting, engineering, law, science, etc., only the graduate school needs to be an "A" school, the one with a reputation for excellence. The undergraduate school can be a "B" school, which is often a state college or university with good programs, albeit larger class size and perhaps fewer food choices in the cafeteria, but with tuition one third the cost of an "A" school. More than one fine surgeon attended a state university before entering Harvard Medical School. Though this idea appeals to parents, I understand our college-bounds are a tough sell, so start planting the seed early. **The message is:** Save your money for graduate school.

4. Financial Safety School

Students enjoy dreaming about their reach-schools, those where they meet the eligibility requirements by standing on their tiptoes, but there's no reason not to try. During this euphoric period, it is also important to select a safety school should life fall apart. This should include a financial safety school that the family can afford should the financial-aid package fall short of what you can afford.

5. Cooperative Education

Some universities offer cooperative education programs where students alternate between classes and a job site. Students work off campus for a salary in an area of interest where two or more students swap roles. Of course, this may extend the amount of time to complete a college degree, but in return you have the money to finish college. You also learn practical job skills, develop contacts for future jobs, and are not burdened with as much debt upon graduation. Compare taking another year to finish college with ten years of debt. Northeastern University in Boston is one of many schools across the country offering this program.

6. Technical Colleges

For some students, technical colleges, not trade schools, could be the way to go. Many programs are completed in two years because you are not taking coursework to complete a bachelor's degree. There are many well-paid professions to choose from. Check the college for employment records. Before enrolling, find students who have graduated and are working. We will always need electricians, automotive technicians, plumbers, appliance repair, and heavy equipment operators. The New England Institute of Technology is one example, and there are others throughout the country. Be wary of for-profit trade schools. Ask lots of questions. Google and Yelp them. Check with the department of education to make sure they are accredited and the Better Business Bureau for complaints that may have been lodged.

7. Community College

Community colleges are an excellent and inexpensive approach to completing the first two years of a four-year degree. This less prestigious and less expensive way of earning two years of credits in a four-year degree program ain't sexy, but it's the best financial deal in town.

8. ROTC Programs - Reserve Officers' Training Corp

If your son or daughter wasn't selected for one of the military academies, there is another way, and it is a good deal. Apply for a ROTC scholarship in your senior year of high school. Students can receive a full or partial scholarship plus money to spend each month while in college. Of course, you obligate yourself to four years' active duty, but it will be in your field, which could be robotics, intelligence, medicine, engineering, electronics, and even meteorology. I have one friend whose son is in Air Force ROTC. They give him a handful of money each month to pay for college. His major is electrical engineering and computer systems. During his years of active duty, not only will he never be in harm's way, but most likely will report to work eight to five like the rest of us.

After completing active duty, there are additional benefits if you agree to stay in the reserves for sixteen or more years. You receive pay grade promotions and a retirement which includes health care insurance for the rest of your life. Our country needs you.

If you like ships and want to make lots of money, try one of our maritime academies. The maritime academy graduates earn as much money out of the gate as graduates from MIT and Harvard. After four years you'll be an officer aboard a merchant ship plying the open seas with nothing out there but a reef or two, a few shipping containers that washed off your deck during a storm, and a handful of pirates wanting to come aboard, none of whom are Johnny Depp.

9. First-Generation Students
Grant money has been set aside by some colleges and private organizations for students who are the first in their family to attend college. Contact the admission office of your prospective college to see if they have support services for first-generation students and ask about special funding. They may transfer you to the finance office to answer your questions.

Go online to "www.firstgenerationstudent.com" or Google "first generation student". Beware of scams.

FAFSA Unique Considerations

The immediate benefit to filling out FAFSA and receiving your Student Aid Report is seeing where the government views you in their scheme of presumed ability to pay for college. Remember the know-thy-enemy-know-thyself paradigm mentioned earlier? The **Student Aid Report** is your passport into the land of federal dollars, including federal loans which you may need if you do not qualify for need-based assistance, state dollars, or private institutional dollars. Without your passport (aka Student Aid Report) you can't get in the country and before any of those uniquely endowed private schools give you a dime, your passport (SAR) is required. Here are eight important FAFSA facts:

1. Double Benefit
Two children attending college at the same time can save you money. This is why. After answering the first 73 questions, they ask, "How many people in your household will be college students?" You answer "2." Your EFC is calculated only once and if the amount is $20,000, it is $20,000 for both, not each of them. With two students in colleges costing $25,000 for one, or $50,000 for two, your total EFC is still only $20,000 which means you are now eligible for a $40,000 Financial Aid Package. To look at this another way, one child gets to go for free. Not really of course, but definitely on paper. If you have two children one year apart, the oldest could take a gap year, earn

some money and go to college with the sibling. If you have triplets, you've struck gold and you deserve a break.

2. Sibling Accounts
Parents and grandparents saving for two or more children to attend college have the potential problem that the total amount could be reported for one child as a FAFSA asset. To prevent this, give each younger child a separate account, to remove those assets from FAFSA. Do you remember what are you going to do with the college-bound student's account before the base year? Right. Put his or her money in a parent account where the assessment is only 5.64 percent.

3. Family-Owned Business
Family-owned businesses with 100 or fewer employees are excluded from the EFC formula. Even a million-dollar business would not be counted. Why? Because you are not expected to sell the business and put your family in financial jeopardy to send your child to college. Family farms are specifically named in this exclusion. So, use the business to pay as many legitimate bills as possible, take a small salary and you will be repaid with a higher financial aid package. You can also pay your son or daughter a salary to work for you, putting the money in savings while deducting a payroll expense.

4. Student Earnings - Income Protection Allowance
Students can earn up to $6,570 (2018) before it is counted as income in the EFC formula. Remember though, if you put the money in savings, 20 percent of the amount is added to the expected family contribution. The best approach is to use the money during the first semester to pay college expenses before December 31, to eliminate student savings in the January FAFSA renewal application. If you need to take excess earnings off the table, look into a Roth IRA which grows tax-free.

5. Work-Study Grants
Student income from a work-study program on campus is not reportable under the federal formula, allowing students to work in summer and earn another $6,570 without any impact on the EFC.

Federal Work-Study grants are the best form of employment during the school year for a student and should never be turned down. When filling out the FAFSA application always check "yes."

6. Grants and Scholarships

Federal grants do not have to be paid back and are often tax-free. Even if the financial aid package doesn't increase, the more grants and scholarships in your financial aid package, the less money you will have to borrow. Pell grants and TEACH grants are two examples.

7. Subsidized Loan

Eligible students can borrow up to $5,500 their freshman year, and additional amounts (6,500 and 7,500) the following years in federal subsidized loans. Students are not charged interest on the loan while they are in school. Often colleges will offer a combination of subsidized and unsubsidized Direct loans in the financial aid package. Talk to your financial aid office about restrictions.

8. Loan Forgiveness

After graduation, if you choose a job in the public sector, e.g. a job working for a town, city, state, or the federal government, the government provides loan forgiveness for federal loans after 120 payments. Ten years beats a lifetime of struggle.

There is another form of loan forgiveness available. If you took out a federal loan to attend a school that promised to teach you a specific trade and you believe that they either failed or that the job availability they promised isn't there, you can request that the federal government forgive your loan. Thousands of students who attended private for-profit schools that went bankrupt and closed down have had their loans forgiven.

> CAUTION: Loan forgiveness does not include money borrowed from banks or other private financial institutions.

Go to the <u>Home Page</u> of our website and click on <u>Financial Charts</u> for a complete list of financial aid and Loan Forgiveness Programs.

9. Simplified Needs Test

If your adjusted gross income is below $49,999, and you file your income tax using form 1040a or 1040EZ, you meet the Department of Education's Simplified Needs Test requirement, which means they will compute your EFC using a "simplified formula" that <u>excludes</u> all assets. One third of college students are independent working adults balancing a college education with a job, home responsibilities, and sometimes a dependent. Many qualify for this exemption. You could have a million-dollar stock portfolio but earn less than $49,999, in which case, your million dollars is off the table.

10. Automatic Zero EFC

If your income is $24,000 or less, and you file your taxes on form 1040a or 1040EZ, FAFSA will compute your <u>Expected Family Contribution</u> to zero. This means the government does not expect you to contribute any income or assets toward paying for college. It does not mean they'll cover the full cost without a loan, however.

Chapter Ten

Financial Planning

Why You Should Save for College

How much does the government expect you to pay for college? Below you will find an Expected Family Contribution Reference Table showing the amount of money you are responsible to pay for college based on adjusted gross income. Call it your college deductible. These are ballpark figures only. You would need to fill out the EFC Formula worksheet from our website to get a real number because adjustments depend upon the state in which you live, your age, federal taxes, and the number in your household. The EFC table below assumes you have one child. If you have more the EFC is lower. If you have less, you're home free.

This is how it works. If you have an AGI (Adjusted Gross Income) of $75,000, the government won't kick in until you reach your $7,394 deductible. The AGI is the amount of money found on line 37 of your 1040. You will need to become familiar with this number because it is required on your FAFSA application.

Expected Family Contribution Reference Table

A.G.I.	E.F.C	% AGI
75,000	7,394	9.9
95,000	13,915	14.6
125,000	23,375	18.7
150,000	30,746	20.5
175,000	38,030	21.7

You can see from the table, the more you make the more you pay. If your AGI is $75,000 you are expected to use 9.9 percent of your money to pay for college. If you earned $150,000 you are expected to use 20.5 percent of earnings but while you may be expected to use 20% of your earnings to pay for college, the federal formula only expects you to use 5.64 percent of your savings.

This is why it pays to save as much as you can. Frugality wins the day. To save enough money to pay for college, how much below your means must you live? Wait. You're asking me to live below my means? Maybe. The Federal Formula assumes you can live below your means by the amount of the expected family contribution shown in the chart above, at least for the four or five years your son or daughter, or both, attend.

For example, with an AGI of $95,000, your EFC is $12,175 or $1,014 a month. If you can afford to live below your means by that much, good for you, but most of us can't. But if you could live below your means by $400 a month for twelve years before your son or daughter begins college, you would have more than enough to cover your Expected Family Contribution. The point is, the sooner you start saving, the easier your job will become..

You can estimate your deductible or EFC the day your child is born if you've got the time. Use the EFC Formula worksheet forms from our website. You can estimate your AGI based on what you think you'll be earning in 18 years. This is a good start to planning for your children's college education.

How much of your savings is protected?

If you have a significant amount of money in the bank, the EFC increases because the government expects you to use that money to pay for college, not buy a new car. Silly you. If you didn't save, or bought the new car, your EFC would decrease slightly. Some parents then say, don't bother saving for college because "they" are going to take it away from you anyway. Let's see how true that is. Look at the Savings Protection chart showing how much of your savings are off the table based upon the age of the oldest adult in the family.

Parents' Education Savings Protection Allowance 2019

Age	Amount	Age	Amount	Age	Amount
44	19,300	49	21,800	54	24,800
45	19,800	50	22,300	55	25,400
46	20,300	51	22,900	56	26,100
47	20,700	52	23,500	57	26,800
48	21,300	53	24,100	58	27,600

So, if you are 48 years old with $50,000 in savings, $21,300 is protected, leaving $28,700 to be assessed at 5.64 percent which is added to your expected family contribution. Have you done the math yet? Your contribution is a paltry $1,619, leaving you with $48,381 left in your savings account. Of course, you might well ask, how do I get $50,000 in my savings account to begin with? See below.

How to Save for College

There are many ways to save and plan for college. I have listed eight of the most interesting ideas we have heard so far. Consult an accountant or financial planner familiar with FAFSA and financial planning for college before you begin.

Here is an important **rule-of-thumb**: You can either save money before your college-bound strolls down the halls of ivy or you can borrow money after your lovely receives his or her acceptance letter, then look forward to 10 or more years of debt and reduced disposable income. Where would you rather be on graduation day?

1. 529 Plans (Qualified Tuition plans)

529 college savings accounts, which refer to the IRS code section, are individual state investment plans run by a state selected financial firm. You hear a lot about 529s because they receive the most publicity and are easy to set up and use. The 529 is owned by the parent or whoever sets up the account for the student (beneficiary). The owner could be someone outside of the household. Advantages include the

beneficiary may be changed if the original student does not go to college, and the generated income from the account is tax free when used for college expenses. Some states allow a tax deduction on a portion of the annual deposit, but when you plug in the numbers, the benefit is often inconsequential.

Disadvantages include the account being treated by a FAFSA as a parent asset. Income from the account not used for college expense is taxed at normal rates and, because the 529 is a mutual fund investment subject to the vagaries of the stock market, the plan could lose money, which has lost money for some parents.

Each state has their own 529 plan, and some of these allow parents from other states to invest. Compare the return and cost of the plan in your state with others. Select the one providing the greatest return on investment.

Read *529 Plans the Flexible Flyer,* and *Ten Best 529 Plans* on our website

2. Series EE and I Savings Bonds have three benefits
   a. They grow tax free. You can purchase them and forget them until your son or daughter needs money to pay for college.

   b. When cashed in they are free from state taxes.

   c. When used for college expenses the interest is not taxed, although it is easy to forget this 18 years later when you cash them in and receive a 1099-INT Savings Bond Redemption report and include as revenue.

3. Whole Life Insurance
A whole life insurance policy taken out when the child is young will yield a guaranteed cash value and a death benefit. The value of a policy for college is twofold. First, the cash value is not considered an

asset by FAFSA and second, you can borrow money from your policy to pay for college. Another important value in insuring your child is the guarantee he or she will not be denied a life insurance policy in the future should they develop a significant medical problem. Later in life, you can transfer ownership of the policy to your son or daughter, who in turn can change the beneficiary to whomever they choose. Just pray it's not a cat. This is double protection. Talk to more than one agent for the best possible rates before you commit. These policies are expensive and require a double dose of due diligence before signing your name on the bottom line.

4. Roth IRA Individual Retirement Accounts

First, the Roth IRA is not counted by FAFSA as an asset. Second, the Roth IRA grows tax-free and the distribution (deposits and interest earned) is tax-free. You can't beat a tax-free income when you are retired. Or make your child the beneficiary, and he or she will be able to inherit the IRA tax-free. Let it grow tax-free and spend it tax-free when they retire, at which time the initial dollars you invested will have grown to a very respectable sum.

To do this you would open a Roth IRA with a custodial agreement that allows you to name a beneficiary (they all do that), a contingent beneficiary in case the first beneficiary predeceases you, and most important a stipulation that allows the beneficiary to extend (stretch) the required minimum distribution (RMD) over his or her lifetime.

You have an additional benefit with the Roth IRA. You can take out the money you put in at any age, you do not have to be 59 1/2, and you can make an early withdrawal up to $10,000 of the interest earned tax-free if the money is used to pay for educational expenses. Just remember, the distribution of funds is considered unearned income by FAFSA. The best use of this money would come after the student has graduated to pay off student loans. The Roth IRA could be a better deal than a 529 plan because the 529 is counted as an asset by FAFSA. Also, in the event your son and daughter is awarded a full scholarship, with the Roth IRA you can keep the money for your retirement without a penalty.

I am not suggesting that you use your retirement IRA to pay for college. That is your retirement money. I am suggesting, however, instead of putting $10,000 into an educational savings account, which is assessed as a FAFSA asset, put the $10,000 in a Roth IRA, which doesn't count as an asset, grows tax-free, and can be withdrawn any time after five years. You can also fund a Roth IRA with gifts from supportive relatives who know the money is going toward a college education. Of course, if your son or daughter did receive that full scholarship, they may want their money back.

Start early. You need to begin putting money into a Roth IRA for college expenses when the children are young because the money cannot be withdrawn for five years after being deposited. When your child turns three, open a Roth IRA depositing $85 dollar a month. You will have reached $10,000 when the child is thirteen. The money sits for five years waiting to be withdrawn tax-free for college expenses. Talk to an accountant.

What do you do with money your son or daughter earns over the limit that would add to your expected family contribution? Consider a Roth IRA. This will also help them develop a healthy respect for planning for the future and living below their means.

5. Traditional IRA

Traditional IRAs are funded with pre-tax money, which lowers your AGI and your taxes. Interest earned is also tax-deferred until you make a withdrawal. Because this IRA lowers your adjusted gross income, this can be an excellent vehicle to reduce your AGI down to $49,999 if you are only a few hundred over that amount. Most important for college financial planning, the IRA is off the table as a FAFSA asset, which increases your demonstrated financial need and hopefully, your financial aid package. Also, the traditional IRA allows you to withdraw $10,000 for education expense before the age of 59 1/2 without a penalty, but remember, this was pre-tax money, so withdrawals are taxed as ordinary income.

6. Pretax Contributions

A note of caution: Pretax contributions to an IRA reduce the adjusted gross income of your tax return and reduce federal and state taxes, but FAFSA considers this untaxed contribution available income you can put toward paying for college. Thus, your untaxed income added to your AGI becomes your Modified Adjusted Gross Income. On the bright side, the federal formula allows you to subtract federal taxes, state taxes, and social security taxes from your EFC. These are the only three expense the formula acknowledges. So... can you take advantage of these rules? Of course, if you haven't maxed out your IRA contribution. Double up on your IRA contribution before the base year to keep your retirement on track which will reduce your taxes. In the base year, make no contributions. This will increase your taxes, which are a deductible FAFSA expense, decreasing your EFC. This is where playing with the EFC Formula worksheet can help you decide your best strategy. The lengths to which some people will go are amazing, aren't they?

7. Stock Market

Invest in the stock market on a monthly basis for 18 years, beginning when your child is born, using the dollar-cost-averaging technique. With this method, you spend a set amount of money each month to buy a balanced fund of stocks and bonds. If stocks are up, you've done well, if they are down, you also do well by buying at a lower price. Over the years, dollar cost averaging works in your favor. Don't pay attention to the daily ups and downs of the market. This is called Quarterly Capitalism and only creates chaos in the market and in your mind, when day traders take their short-term profits and run. For the rest of us, set it and forget it! If that frightens you, however, purchase exchange-traded funds, which are a bucket of stocks replicating the market's growth. You could earn enough money to pay for college and buy a yacht.

Really? That works? No. Not always. Timing is everything. If your son or daughter attends college when the S&P is up, lucky you. If they are attending when the market tanks, you're toast, plain and simple.

If you had bought a hundred shares of Microsoft twenty-five years ago when they went public, those shares would be worth three-quarters of a million dollars today. What? You didn't do that? Me neither. That's why I'm filling out FAFSA so my daughter can attend the college of "our" mutually agreed-upon choice. And speaking of mutual...

8. Mutual Funds

Mutual funds are an easy way to invest without worrying about which stocks or bonds to buy. All you must do is pick a sector. You can read the advertisements or go online and find a mutual fund that appeals to you. But remember this.

Mutual funds are a box of stocks and bonds bought and sold by a well-paid fund manager. Becoming a fund manager, by the way, is not a bad career choice. The money to pay the manager comes from the same box containing your stocks and bonds and is considered an operating cost. Operating costs include office expenses, staff payroll, advertising expenses, trips, bonuses, cleaning, and cappuccino machines. These expenses cost 1 to 1.5 percent of your assets each year which, of course, reduces your net assets by that same amount That means for your dollars to keep up with the stock market, your fund would need to grow 1 to 1.5 percent more than the market to break even. When the sales representative tells you how much the fund has earned in the last year, remember that is how much the company earned, not the shareholders.

But Wait, There's More

Some of the ideas mentioned here may not apply to you or seem off the grid; however, if you have the opportunity, like I did, to sit around the campfire with a few creative minds, brainstorming the many ways to reduce your expected family contribution before the first tuition bill arrives in the mail, you may come up with additional ideas of your own. If so, we'd love to hear them. We discussed everything from buying exotic sport cars to marrying off our daughters for a fee. The opportunities described above range from innovative to old school and under the right circumstance, actually work. If nothing else, it stretches the mind. Good Luck.

> **Be Forewarned.** All financial products have three elements in common. **1**. they are designed by people to make money for their company, **2**. they are sold by people who earn a living from the money we give them, and **3**. you and I are nothing more than a byproduct of the product they sell.

Basic Financial Strategies

The base year is the line in the sand. FAFSA collects financial information from your income tax return covering the base year which begins January 1 of the college-bound student's junior year in high school. Your job is to reduce your adjusted gross income and your assets before that year is up. For example, if you are in line for bonuses, stock options, or other extra income, if possible, elect to receive them before the base year or when your college-bound student is a high school sophomore. The following are five short-term financial strategies.

1. Assets in Student's Name
Student's assets include: savings accounts, certificates of deposit, savings bonds, stock portfolio, and trusts. You or your relatives may have set up one of these accounts in your child's name to save for their college education. Good for you, but the government wants that money. Student savings are assessed at a rate of 20 percent, meaning 20 percent of the money will be added to the expected family contribution (EFC) each year. In contrast, parents' assets first have a protection allowance after which the remainder is assessed at the lower rate of 5.64 percent.

The message is clear. Keep assets out of the student's name.

> **Rule of Thumb:** Every thousand dollars transferred
> from student's savings to parents' savings reduces
> the Expected Family Contribution by $143.60.

2. Asset Reduction

A Pay off Debts. There is a way to remove assets from the table and increase your monthly cash flow without increasing your adjusted gross income. The EFC Formula includes savings, but not your primary residence as an asset. You can take assets off the table by paying off your mortgage and credit card debt. This will reduce your EFC, reduce your monthly living expenses, and increase your federal aid. Remember Adam and Eve?

B Retirement Funds are not counted as an asset. Another way to take assets off the table is to increase the funding of your IRA or 401(k) if you are not at maximum level. For large amounts of money, purchasing an **annuity** is an option. For example, if you are six years away from age 59 1/2 you could purchase a fixed-rate five-year annuity with no fees. It works like a CD, but it is a retirement program, which takes the money off the table in the FAFSA calculation. When your son or daughter finishes college, take the money back with no penalty or tax on your initial deposit as long as you are 59 1/2. Contact an investment advisor or accountant for the best plan for you before putting up with a sales pitch from an insurance or investment broker.

C Additional Asset Exclusions. FAFSA does not include the following assets in the federal aid formula: personal belongings including antique furniture, priceless work of art, sports cars, boats, and planes. These assets could add up to a million dollars and not be counted. You would not be expected to sell any of them to pay for college. The opportunities to shelter your money can be lots of fun. Less fun, but more practical, is taking money off the table by accelerating expenses coming up in the next year or two. Purchase the needed car, paint the house, or install the new roof before you go online and fill out and submit your FAFSA. You might be thinking, I could fill in FAFSA with any numbers I want, how would they know? There are red flags reviewers find easy to spot, and one third are audited.

3. Asset Protection of Savings

Savings accounts, certificates of deposit, savings bonds, and brokerage accounts not owned by anyone in the household are off the table in the FAFSA federal formula. Grandparents or other relatives could own these savings with the intention of using the money to pay for college. This can work well if the money does not pass through either parent or the student, making the funds reportable as untaxed income. Be warned, however, if someone outside the family sends a large check to the college for tuition, the college may ask some questions and end up reducing the financial aid package by an equal amount. Here are some workarounds.

Grandma pays the student for work on her property and as long as the student's total income does not exceed $6,570 in one year, this is fine. And when you get the check, spend it for college. Don't put the money in savings. If there is a lot of money involved, grandma can write the check after the student graduates to help pay off the loans. That's about as good a graduation gift as anyone could receive.

4. Asset Protection of Second Home

Your second and third, etc. home is counted as an asset. You can reduce the asset by using this property to take out a home equity line of credit (HELOC) to pay for college. The money borrowed reduces the equity and your EFC. Another option is to create a real estate irrevocable trust (REIT) to remove the house from the table or include the property in a family-owned business. Note: rental property is considered an investment, not a business, and remains on the table.

The second house is also off the table if ownership is in legal dispute or there is a substantial lien against the property.

Alternatively, you can sell the home and put the money into a retirement annuity as described earlier.

5. Adjusted Gross Income Reduction

If you ever wanted to start a small part-time business, now is the time. You will most likely incur a paper loss for the first two or three years, which is expected by the IRS. This will lower your AGI and increase your demonstrated financial need. Stay-at-home moms or dads could sell items on eBay, for example. Go to the IRS website and search for a PDF of "Schedule C." This is the schedule used to report profit and loss of a small business. Part II provides a list of expenses that can be deducted from your income. Vehicles, travel, and meals are on the list. Be careful and expect an audit.

You will find *Schedule C* on our website under this chapter in the Book Resources section.

Chapter Eleven

2018 Tax Bill

The Good, The Bad, The Okay

The 2018 tax bill signed into law is designed to lower taxes for corporations and high-income families as well as impact the average American family to a lesser degree. The major provisions relating to parents with college and college-bound students is described below. If you would like to read the 1,097-page tax bill, it is located on our website, www.survivingthecostofcollege.com.

The Good Increased Standard Deduction
Personal and family deductions will be doubled under the new law. This is the amount of money deducted from earnings before we are taxed. In 2017, the deduction for married couples filing jointly was $12,700. In 2018, the standard deduction becomes $24,000 for joint filers, which further reduces your taxable income. That's the good news.

The Bad No Exemptions
1. Last year parents could deduct $4,050 for each person living in their home. If there are two parents and one child, the deduction is $12,150. In 2018, these exemptions are eliminated. For a family of three, the loss of the exemption is made up for by the increased standard deduction. For each additional child, however, parents lose $4,050. Some of this could be offset by the Child Tax Credit **(CTC)** of $2,000 per child under the age of 17 for qualifying taxpayers.

2. The second bad is that the present administration has pledged to cut **four billion dollars** from federal aid including work-study programs and federal Direct loans with rates at 5.05 percent plus an origination fee. This would push millions of college students into borrowing money from the private sector that charges 11 percent or more in interest depending upon your credit rating. Here is the difference.

Private vs. Federal Loan of $20,000 for 10 years

	Rate	Payment	Interest
Private Loan	11.0%	$275	$13,060
Federal Loan	5.05%	$213	$5,514
	Difference	$62	$7,546

The difference of $62 a month may not seem like a lot, but remember, that's $62 a month for ten years. Paying an additional $7,546 in interest, however should get your attention.

Unfortunately, this is already a reality for millions of students who have to borrow more money than is available through the federal aid program.

The Okay for Some but not All

In 2017 the taxable income of a large majority of families filing joint returns ranged between $75,901 and $153,100, which is the old 25% tax bracket. In 2018 that bracket changes to between $77,400 and $165,000 and is now taxed at 22 percent. If you want a quick check on how you will fair in 2018, look at <u>line 37</u> of your 2017 1040 tax return. This is your <u>Adjusted Gross Income</u> (AGI) and is a number you will need to use when filling out FAFSA. If you are married filing a joint return and do not itemize, subtract $24,000. This is your new Taxable Income. Using paper, pencil apply this formula.

Multiply the amount of your taxable income that is over $77,400 by 22% (.22) then add $8,907. This is your estimated tax responsibility. Compare that number with the number on <u>line 44</u> of your 1040 to see how much you saved. These numbers work for married couples filing a joint return and do not include tax credits.

If your income did not fall within $77,4000 to $165,000 range, or you filed under a different status, you would need to use a different tax table. These are available on our website under "Book Resources."

Three points

a. If you are fortunate enough to pay less taxes, this counts against you when filling out FAFSA. The more taxes you report on your application (line 86 in the print version), the more eligible you become to receive federal grants and loans, and vice versa. Though, if I had to choose between the two, I'd select paying lower taxes.

b. Reducing taxes reduces the amount of money the government has available to spend, which increases the amount of money the feds must borrow to run the country and in turn increase the national debt that your college student will have to pay in the future.

c. These tax changes are only good for <u>eight years</u>, after that they could revert back to the old rate, which means your good fortune is good for the duration of an 8-year presidency, after which the next Commander in Chief gets to pay the piper.

Social Security Non-Taxable Income

If a family member is receiving social security retirement benefits and has or is taking care of a child under the age of 18, that child is entitled to a social security benefit equal to 1/2 of the family member's benefit. This money must be spent on the welfare of the child and is often used to create a college savings account. This income is not taxed.

More and more parents are raising their grandchildren. Social Security will pay benefits to grandchildren when the grandparents retire. The children's parents must be deceased or disabled, or the grandchild must be adopted by the grandparent.

Lost Tax Deductions

Six tax deductions no longer available under the 2018 tax bill.

1 Personal Exemption: Your 2017 personal exemption of $4,050 deducted from your adjusted Gross Income is gone.

2 Miscellaneous Itemized Deductions: Job search expenses, unreimbursed work expenses, gambling losses, investment expenses and tax preparation fees, exceeding 2% of adjusted gross income are gone.

3 Moving Expenses: Moving expenses are no longer deductible unless you are member of the armed forces on active duty.

4 Dependent Exemption: The 2017 dependent exemption of $4,050 for someone you are supporting is no longer available. This typically occurs when you are supporting children living in your home who are over the age of eighteen.

5 Personal Casualty and Theft Losses: such as fires, storms, and thefts are currently considered an itemized deduction (above the 10% adjusted gross income threshold). Beginning in 2018, this tax deduction only remains for casualties incurred in a Federally-declared disaster.

6 Charitable Contributions: Itemized tax deductions will most likely not add up to the increased standard deduction of $12,000 for single, and $24,000 for married filing jointly. This is estimated to have a significant impact on charitable organizations including colleges that rely on alumni donations.

Tax Credits

1. Child Tax Credit

The child tax credit, which is deducted directly from taxes owed, has been increased to $2,000 per child under the age of 17. This phases out for single parents with income over $200,000 and married couples filing jointly at $400,000. This is a refundable tax credit, which means if the tax credit is greater than the taxes owed, some of that money is reimbursed to the parents.

2. Child and Dependent Care Tax Credit

Parents who are paying someone else to take care of their child under the age of 13, or a spouse or dependent age 13 and over if they are physically or mentally incapable of caring for themselves, can take a tax credit of between 20% and 35% of up to $3,000 in expenses paid for each dependent.

3. Adoption Tax Credit

Parents or individuals adopting a child can take a tax credit of up to $13,570 per child, which begins to phase out for families with incomes over $203,540. While these credits are non-refundable, they can be carried over for up to six years. Costs that can be claimed for this tax credit include adoption fees, attorney fees, court costs, travel expenses including meals and lodging, and re-adoption expenses relating to expenses in foreign countries. These credits significantly reduce the cost of adoption, allowing parents an increased opportunity to begin a college saving account.

4. Earned Income Credit (EIC)

If you are a single parent earning less than $39,617 and have one child, you are eligible to receive a maximum tax credit of $3,400. With two or more children and income less than $45,007, the maximum credit increases to $5,616. This credit is deducted from your tax bill.

Tuition Costs Tax Benefits

There are four specific tax benefits designed to reduce the cost of college for families and independent students that are part of the Federal Higher Education Student Aid program and are touted to provide an estimated 36 billion dollars in relief to parents of 11 million students attending college. By way of comparison, in case you are interested, the federal government provides up to 775 billion in subsidies to the fossil fuel industry. Now you know where our children stand compared to a gallon of oil and a lump of coal.

These four tax benefits are grouped in two categories: (1) tax deductions that are subtracted from earned income to reduce the adjusted gross income (AGI), and (2) tax credits that are subtracted from taxes owed to the government. This is the best deal if you have that option.

1. Student Loan Interest Deduction. Line 33 of your 1040 allows you to deduct the interest you paid on your college loan up to $2,500. The amount you can deduct is reduced or eliminated based on your Adjusted Gross Income. Filing single, head of household, you cannot take this deduction if your AGI is over $75,000 or over $150,000 for married filing joint return.

2. Tuition and Fees Deduction. Line 34 of your 1040 allows you to deduct up to $4,000 of your tuition and fees. The amount you can deduct is reduced or eliminated based on your Adjusted Gross Income. If filing single, head of household, you cannot take this deduction if your AGI is over $80,000 or over $160,000 if married filing joint return. You must attach form 8917.

3. Lifetime Learning Credit. Line 50 of your 1040 allows a credit for 20 percent of qualified undergraduate and graduate expenses of one or more students in the household up to $2,000 per tax return. Compare this with the American Opportunity Credit, which may provide a larger amount. This credit is not available if filing single and your AGI is over $60,000 or $120,000 if married filing jointly. You must attach form 8863 and use line 19 of this form on your tax return.

4. American Opportunity Credit. Line 68 of your 1040 allows a credit of up to $4,000 of college expense. (Note: This pertains only to expenses paid with cash or student loan money, not federal aid.) You receive 100% of the first $2,000 and 25% of the next $2,000 for a maximum credit of $2,500 per student. $1,000 is refundable if you have no tax burden. This tax credit is not available if filing single and your AGI is over $90,000 or $180,000 if married filing jointly. You must attach form 8863. Use line 8 of this form on your tax return. Ask your accountant.

Two Points to Remember

Parents can only access these tax benefits if they claim the student on their federal income tax return, and while you can deduct up to $2,500 in interest paid on federal education loans, you cannot deduct the interest paid on private loans.

Watch List

They Did Do This

The 2018 tax bill does impose a new tax on college endowments which consist of money donated by alumni and others to either support future growth (buildings and programs) or support students with scholarships. Endowment funds are invested to provide a steady stream of income to support programs and students. The new "excise" tax now charges 1.4 percent on net investment income on private colleges and universities with endowments valued at $500,000 or more per student. Just as some in congress criticize private colleges for not providing more scholarship money for students in need, they pass legislation that reduces the amount of scholarship money that would be available for this purpose.

They Almost Did This

We think of the tax bill as a reduction in corporate and individual taxes. But the bill also included new revenues to reduce the deficit the tax bill created. Students working on their graduate degrees in the sciences take classes, engage in independent research projects, and either teach a class or assist a professor teaching a class. The workload is not for the faint of heart. For the student's contribution to the school, the colleges usually waive the cost of tuition. Congress included in their bill a requirement that students would pay a tax on the waived tuition, in effect taxing students on money they did not receive. The purpose of this section of the bill was to recoup some of the financial loss incurred by tax reductions elsewhere in the bill.

As soon as this provision became known, the schools and the graduate students from across the country spoke to their congressional representatives, some of whom were not aware of this section, resulting in the provision being removed from the tax bill.

They Are Looking to do This

Looming on the horizon is the White House proposal to cut 4 billion in annual funding from the student aid program The would eliminate public service loan forgiveness provision, end subsidized loans, eliminate the Supplemental Education Opportunity Grants (SEOG) for low income students, and cut Work-Study grants in half.

Our website will keep you up to date on these proposals.

Chapter Twelve

Borrowing Money

Millions of hard-working families barely earn enough money to pay their mortgage on a modest home, keep food on the table, afford health insurance and out-of-pocket medical bills, and pay for gas to drive to work. There is little, or no money left for savings. Our next college-bound student has decided to follow in his father's footsteps and become a teacher. He chooses an in-state public school within commuting distance, so he can live at home to save the expense of room and board. Tuition is $8,776. This does not include books and transportation. The parents are teachers and earn a total of $70,000 of which FAFSA says the Expected Family Contribution, or deductible, is $9,000, which turns out to be more than the tuition cost of their son's school.

Because their savings were spent on family medical bills, they had no choice but to borrow $9,000 for each year he was in college. At seven percent interest, the monthly payment for a ten-year loan is $104.50. The monthly payment for the full $36,000 (4 times 9,000) is $418. The total cost of the loan is $36,000 in principal and $14,159 in interest, or 38 percent of the amount borrowed over a ten-year period. Once our young teacher subtracts that monthly payment from his first-year teacher's salary, he will not have enough money left to live independently and save for a down payment on a home. Because banks include student loans in the buyer's debt-to-income ratio (DTI), he most likely would not receive a mortgage, even if he had the money for a down payment. Pulling yourself up by your bootstraps, the American way, has become all but impossible with the weight of college debt on your shoulders.

If our future teacher misses a payment for any reason, his FICO credit score will be lowered, resulting in paying a higher interest rate on a loan for a car or anything else purchased on time. And because the House Committee on Education and Workforce created legislation that excluded student loans from being discharged in bankruptcy, should our teacher suffer a financial devastation, he would have to put up with a debt collector's constant barrage of threatening phone calls and letters. If you think the lending agencies really care about students, no matter how friendly their website, you haven't met their debt collectors. Admittedly, this is a worst-case scenario, but bankruptcy resulting from not being able to pay medical bills is a worst-case scenario for 1.5 million Americans every year.

On a national level, the purpose of a college education is to make America strong and competitive with other countries. The roadblock to higher education is not student ability or willingness to do more. The roadblock is the excessive profits of financial institutions backed by congressional capitulation and subsequent regulation to strip every dime from the student's pocket in exorbitant interest rates and fees. Here is one example: The 2015-2016 FAFSA Table A5 provides a savings allowance for a 45-year-old parent of $28,200. In calculating the family expected contribution to pay for college, $28,200 of savings is protected. Off the table. The 2018-2019 Table 5A shows the protected allowance has been **reduced** to $19,800. This is a protection loss of $8,400. This loss will increase the amount of money families will have to pay for their sons and daughters to attend college and more significantly, increase the amount of money a family will have to borrow, which creates more profit for the banks.

Federal Loans under FAFSA include: Direct Loans, subsidized and unsubsidized, and PLUS loans. The college will most likely include one of these loans in the student's financial package. If a gap exists between the financial package and what the student and parent can afford to pay for college, that unmet need may be filled with a second Parent Loan for Undergraduate Students (PLUS) loan. The PLUS loan is also federally financed, and the application is made through the college financial aid office. The interest rate for PLUS loans 2019 is 7.6 percent plus a 4.264 origination fee.

The Bipartisan Student Loan Certainty Act of 2013 ties interest rates to the high yield of the ten-year treasury note auctioned prior to June 1. This is helpful when the interest rates are down, but not when they go up. The Congressional Budget Office estimated that the government **profits** on student loans will increase by $715 million over the next 11 years. That's right. The government is making a profit on your children. You remember the saying I'm from the government and I'm here to help you? They are here to help remove money from your pocket.

Private Loans

Private loans are usually second loans, which means you are already making one monthly payment. If a student took out a direct loan for 5,000 a year for four years, that $20,000 would cost $218 a month. If the student needed to take out a PLUS loan of $20,000 to fill the gap, at 7% plus the origination fee, that loan would cost an additional $232 a month, bringing the total up to $450 a month.

Sallie Mae is the nation's largest private student loan provider. They loan money at rates from 7 percent to 12 percent and up depending upon your credit rating. The lower your credit score, the higher the interest rate. If the student borrowed $6,000 from Sallie Mae at their interest rate of 12 percent for ten years, each $6,000 would cost $86 a month. Google "college loan calculator" and several will come up. Choose one and you can play the "what if" game.

Sallie Mae offers a program that, in the case of emergency, allows you to postpone payments for a year or two until you are back on your feet. The interest you would normally pay, of course, continues to accrue and is added to the monthly payment. Also, during the non-payment period you will be obligated to make a payment of at least $50.00 a month which is not deducted from your loan. This is called a forbearance option.

There are alternatives to Sallie Mae. You can borrow from the cash value of life insurance policies, stock market margin accounts, 401k accounts and IRA accounts if you have these options. If not...

HELOCs

You can also borrow money from the bank on the equity (net value) of your home. With a Home Equity Line of Credit (HELOC), you only pay interest on the money you use after writing a check to the college. The variable interest rate you pay is based on the present prime rate, your credit rating, and the amount you borrow. The maximum line of credit is 70 percent or less of the net value of your home based on the bank's property inspection. If you do take out a HELOC, there are two ways to pay it back.

The first is to write a check from your Home Equity line of credit account each year in the amount you need to cover the financial gap and pay back the loan over ten years or a shorter period. (You can pay a HELOC loan off at any time.) This is dicey because the variable interest rate will invariably go up. The second way is to pay off the amount you borrow in one year of monthly payments instead of ten. A $6,000 loan would cost about $520 a month and would be paid off in twelve months. If the family can reduce spending or increase income in the amount of the loan payment, the debt will be discharged at the end of the year. Upon graduation, this method eliminates thousands of dollars in student debt as well as ten years of anxiety and lost opportunity to put that money to much greater use.

Local Banks

No matter what avenue you end up taking, we recommend looking closer to home. There is a good chance that your bank, or a bank in your state, offers student loans at very reasonable rates.

Chapter Thirteen

Revocable Trusts for Protection

Two friends traveled through life with the same amount of financial success. One day, it was time to travel on, so each wrote out a will and dumped his belongings into a backpack.

Tommy Jones wrote his name on his backpack, so everyone would know that everything inside belonged to him. The contents included money for his children and grandchildren to attend college. His backpack read: "Owned by Tommy Jones." His friend, Harry Smith, decided to create a revocable trust into which he placed all his assets, which also included funds to pay for college. His backpack read "Owned by the Trust of Harry Smith."

When the two friends reached the border, the gatekeepers read Tommy's will and asked him to open his backpack for inspection. They asked how much his car and house were worth, the value of his stocks, mutual funds, CDs, college savings accounts, and checking. Tommy wasn't sure about the house and car and said he'd have to send for statements on everything else. "Call this lawyer," they said, "and he'll get everything appraised, so we'll know how much tax you owe us. The lawyer won't cost you more than six hundred dollars." "How long will that take?" asked Tommy. "Six months if all goes well," they said. "So, who pays the bills on my property after I'm gone?" "You must have some relatives who can do that," they replied. Tommy saw dark clouds ahead for his survivors.

Harry Smith was next. He handed them his last will and testament that read, I give the residue of my estate to my trust. They filed Harry's will, handed him his backpack and told him to have a nice journey. Everything in Harry Smith's backpack now belonged to the successor trustee he had named, who was free to distribute Harry's assets, including money to pay for college, with no waiting period or expense.

I have always considered that one of my most important jobs is to protect our daughter from harm, then, through example and conversation, provide the tools she would need to advocate for herself, become thoughtful and independent, find happiness, and become financially secure through prudent and rational decision-making.

Unfortunately, or fortunately, depending upon your point of view, this job also includes planning for her future when neither my wife nor I will be here. This comes under the heading of parents **not** making life difficult or stressful for their children, especially during periods of grief. How did we do that?

Like Harry Smith, we created a revocable trust. Upon our passing, our daughter, as a successor trustee, will have full rights to access and manage the assets in the trust without involving probate court. In fact, our daughter will be able to fill out and submit a simple one page "no asset" form to probate court along with our original last will and testament, death certificate, a copy of the paid funeral bill, and a check for $34.00. Our daughter will be able to continue attending college and get on with her life without hiring an attorney or being tied up in probate court. This, by the way, is all I had to do when my mother passed away. Fortunately for her children, she kept her trust up-to-date, making life easier for all of us.

> The most important advantage to having a revocable trust
> is <u>continuity</u>. Properly funded, the trust will continue to
> pay college expenses without interruption or interference
> from the court should something happen to you.

To create a trust, your first job is to find an attorney you like, feel confident in, and won't charge an arm and a leg. There are plenty around, so stay away from the others. Most attorneys provide a free, one-hour consultation which you should look upon as an interview. Unless you are fully convinced, and hopefully not totally taken in, wait a few days before making your decision. At that meeting, the attorney should tell you what they charge for developing your wills, a revocable trust, and for preparing and recording a quitclaim deed to place your home and other real estate into your trust.

Each state has different rules for creating wills and trusts and only a lawyer who practices in your state will be able to prepare the documents you will need to meet those requirements. However, they all take on essentially the same form and meet the same purpose in every state.

Revocable or Living Trusts

A revocable trust is a legal document that **first**, specifies you have complete control over your assets during your lifetime and **second**, that your selected successor trustee, not the court, will distribute your assets as described in the trust after your death.

Deciding how to distribute your assets can become the most difficult part of creating a trust, because you must choose who gets what, and in the case of something unforeseen happening to one of those people, what changes you would make. This becomes a what-if game of the highest order, but there is one important saving factor not to be overlooked. You can amend (change) your trust at any time. In fact, you should review your trust every three to five years to make sure it fits your present circumstances. For example, once your child or children reach the age of majority and are formerly established, you may amend the trust to include them as an executor, or even a settlor, which means the trust continues without disruption.

Once the trust is completed, you must fund it. Without making the trust the owner of your assets, it is of no value. Think of your trust as a castle built to protect you from predators, in this case, probate court. You've got to bring your assets across the moat and through the castle gate to be sheltered. You can begin by going to the bank and requesting they put your savings, CDs, etc. into your trust. They will make a copy of the trust document for their records, change the account name on their computer, and you're done. The process is quick and easy. You continue to have full power over that account. You can put money in and take it out as nothing ever changed. Your attorney should have already put your real estate into the trust with a quitclaim deed.

Five advantages of a revocable trust

AVOID PROBATE. Assets do not go through probate, avoiding time and expense.

PRIVACY. There is no public record of the assets in a trust.

FLEXIBILITY. Allows you to include out-of-state individuals and assets without worrying about individual state laws.

CONTINUITY. There is no interruption in managing and dispensing of funds.

AVAILABILITY. Property in the trust is available for immediate liquidation.

IMPORTANT. To protect the money you set aside to pay for college, those accounts and plans (529s, etc.) should be put into the trust. This will allow the successor trustee to continue funding your son's or daughter's college education without interruption.

Documents: There are actually five documents you will want prepared for you.

1. Pour-over wills for each spouse that state your assets are held by the trust.
2. Revocable or Living Trust
3. Quitclaim deed that puts your property into the trust
4. Health Care Power of Attorney for each spouse
5. Financial Power of Attorney for each spouse

The importance of planning ahead to fund a college education and to protect those assets cannot be overstated. A revocable trust becomes a powerful tool to continue funding a college education for your children, making life easier for them later.

Taking advantage of this simple, inexpensive legal instrument to ensure that your financial wishes for your children and grandchildren are carried out after you are gone is amazing when you think about it, since they certainly aren't carried out when we're alive.

My Personal Experience

As I mentioned earlier, my mother's last will and testament took no time at all to file, but what is not often made clear is that upon the death of the trustee (owner of the trust), the trust goes from being revocable to irrevocable and requires its own tax ID number for the IRS to track-and-tax the sale of property or other assets put in that trust. In our case, my mother's trust owned the home and would be the seller of the home. Now we needed a checking account in the name of the trust into which the proceeds could be deposited. The attorney who created the trust could take care of that for you or you could go online to the IRS website where you can do it for free. The easiest way to find this website is to Google "apply for IRS EIN number" or you can call 888-321-6690 and do it over the phone. I went online.

The online form was easy to fill out. The IRS assigned a 9-digit employee identification number (EIN) for my mother's trust, and I hit print. The entire process took less than five minutes. My wife and I brought the two-page EIN certificate to the bank along with my mother's trust, and 15 minutes later the trust had its own checking account. The trust was now a separate legal entity subject to IRS rules and regulations

Chapter Fourteen

Good Schools with Low Tuition Rates

D id you ever wonder why parents are willing to pay $20, $30, $40 or $50,000 a year for their son or daughter to take twelve classes a year, live in a cramped dorm room, and eat questionable food? Many do because they think they have to, and colleges charge these grand amounts because they have more applications than slots to fill, creating an owner's market. But that is not the case everywhere.

Not all colleges fill their freshman slots or maintain their upper-class enrollment. With over 600 public institutions and 1800 private institutions to choose from and the number of 18-to-24-year-old high schoolers on the decline, the inevitable is out there.

Moody's Investor Services rates the financial health of colleges and universities. They report that, on average, at least three colleges close every year and another two or more merges with, or are bought out by, another school. Daniel Webster College merged with Southern New Hampshire University, Wheelock College in Boston merged with Boston University, and U-Mass Dartmouth just bought Mt. Ida College in Newton, Massachusetts, lock, stock and barrel. Other schools just close their doors. The well-known historical Sweet Briar College in Virginia announced they were closing their doors in 2015. The New York Times reported, "The abrupt decision this month by the Sweet Briar board to close the 114-year-old women's liberal arts school at the end of this term as a result of insurmountable financial challenges with no advance warning to students, parents, alumnae, or professors has transformed this tranquil community into a hotbed of anger and activism." The Times also noted that fifty years ago there were 250 women's colleges and today that number is down to 45.

Why is this Important to You?
Well, of course the first step is to select a college that is not on the ropes and there are many ways to do that. Secondly, many colleges keep up their enrollment by reducing their tuition rates. The University of Maine's flagship campus located in Orono, up the road a piece from Bangor, has opened its doors to qualifying out-of-state students at the same tuition rate charged to in-state students. That could be a savings of up to $14,000 a year.

Other colleges have recently announced tuition reductions. Utica College in Utica, New York has lowered their tuition by 42% and Rosemont College in Rosemont, Pennsylvania by 41%. Some colleges in Washington state are reducing their tuition by 5% which is not a lot, but tuition is already low in many cases.

Best Value Schools provides a list of the 100 most affordable colleges in America. Choose the tuition range you can afford and a list of schools will come up for your review. Scrolling down, I found my graduate school alma mater, West Virginia University, with an in-state tuition of $8,976 and an out-of-state tuition of $25,056. The out-of-state tuition is a jump, but still a good financial deal for the programs offered by this internationally known university. *Did you know it was WVU engineer Dan Carder who led the research team that discovered Volkswagen was cheating on their emissions tests?*

Go to **www.bestvalueschools.com**, or Google best value schools and you will find a continuously updated list of schools you can afford. If you know what you can afford, they provide quick links to lists of schools by a range of tuition rates from under $16,000 per year to under $3,000 per year.

One of the least expensive and most interesting schools I found was Berea College in Berea, Kentucky. Berea is a tuition-free work college ranked 76th best liberal arts school by U.S. News. They have thirty-three courses of study and one of the highest per capita endowments in the country. Berea is in southern Kentucky, off Route 75 south of

Lexington and a short drive to the 700,000-acre Daniel Boone National Forest that spreads over 21 counties.

The best colleges and even the not-so-best can charge a princely sum, but if you can get over not attending the Ivies or other "top" schools in the country, there are many more that provide a solid four-year education at prices too good to refuse.

For additional ways to pay lower or no tuition at top notch international colleges and universities read *Going to School in Canada* and *An Overseas Education* column on our website.

Chapter Fifteen

For-Profit Schools

Private for-profit schools provide a quick hands-on approach to earning a certificate or degree in everything from computer technology to driving trucks. You may find a future somewhere among the career choices they offer. Six to eighteen months beats four years of college and taking freshman English and history courses that have no relevance to your career. So, the quick hands-on approach makes sense. Right? The answer is an absolutely qualified.... maybe.

A good part of the trillion-dollar debt problem is the result of students attending for-profit trade schools and not getting the training they need or the jobs they expected after completing the program. For-profit trade schools are a buyer-beware proposition. Schools have closed their doors in the middle of the year, leaving students without their promised degree, jobless and with student loan debt. I don't mean to scare you but, no wait, I do. Corinthian Colleges, Inc., one of the country's largest for-profit college chains, shut down their remaining two dozen schools in 2015, leaving 16,000 students stranded. The story is much sadder than portrayed here and is worth researching. Even though the government has oversight and knew that Corinthian was being sued or investigated by several states' attorneys general, they did not protect the student or the taxpayer by closing them down, allowing millions in federal dollars (your taxes) to keep them afloat even while they were beyond repair and headed for bankruptcy.

So, before you apply to a for-profit trade school, make sure they are well established, not under investigation, and plan to be around for the long haul. And, by the way, you might ask yourself if your career choice is even realistic.

First, learn about the career you selected. What are the job duties? What is the starting pay? Where are these jobs today? Where will this job lead in five years? **Second**, go online and do a job search. Assume you graduated. Where would you go for an interview? **Third**, go to businesses that employ people in your prospective field and ask them if your degree will get you in the door; and **Fourth**, ask the for-profit trade school for a list of businesses that have hired their graduates in your future profession.

If your career choice includes opening your own business, remember being an entrepreneur is hard, time-consuming work requiring a boat load of stamina, organizational skills and luck. Only one in five new businesses succeed, and even those require three to five years to turn a profit. If you can write a business plan, know how to read a balance sheet and have someone to support you for five years, you have a 20 percent chance of being successful. Good luck.

When visiting a for-profit school, ask these questions.

1. Is the school accredited? Check online at: www.nces.ed.gov.
2. Is the school partnered with businesses for hands-on training?
3. Does the school have employment support services?

When you tour the facility, check out the location. Is the neighborhood safe? Is the inside of the building clean and well lit? Are the bathrooms clean? Ask for the student withdrawal rate and the graduating students' employment rate, student teacher ratio and the background/training of the instructors. Ask what they did before they started teaching, and how they are certified or licensed?

If you believe you have been defrauded, there is a federal law that forgives student debt of federal loans if the borrowers can prove their school used illegal tactics to recruit them. This would include false claims of employment and inflated salary opportunities upon graduation.

Having said all that, there are some excellent for-profit schools out there. Just do your homework first!

Chapter Sixteen

Independent Student

The driving force within the federal formula that calculates the amount of need-based financial aid for <u>Dependent</u> college students is the parent's and the student's annual income. If the student is reclassified as <u>Independent</u>, however, only his or her income is considered.

In chapter six we described Mary Smith, a Dependent student living at home with her parents, with an Expected Family Contribution (EFC) of 12,715. If Mary were to become an Independent student and earning, for example, $32,000 a year, her expected family contribution would be down to $8,700, which could increase her financial aid by another $4,000. And remember, under the FAFSA formula, savings and other assets of individuals or families with income under $49,000, are not included in the calculation.

To receive this designation however, Mary would have to become a *Financially Independent Student*, <u>fully responsible for her room, board and living expenses.</u>

Some students live at home, contribute to household expenses and pay for their college education. In this case they may ask the college to be considered an Independent student by applying for a <u>Dependency Override</u>.

The first step is to fill out a <u>Dependency-Review Form</u> available at the college's financial-aid office. Each school has their own, and probably no two are alike. After filling out the form you would meet with an administrator for an interview, who's decision is final.

To give you an idea of what constitutes consideration for reclassification, which one of the following situations, would you guess, is reason enough for the financial aid administrator to authorize a dependency override? Parents refuse to pay for college, parents refuse to provide information to fill out FAFSA. Parents do not claim the student on their income tax. The answer is, none of them.

Conditions considered for an override include: an abusive family environment with a court order against the parents, abandonment by the parents, and incarceration or institutionalization of both parents. Let us hope that none of these is ever the reason for you to request an override.

The generally accepted ways to become a financially independent student in the eyes of the college or university is to meet one or more of the following eight established criteria.

1. Be 24 years of age or older by December 31 of the award year
2. Be an orphan, ward of the court, or in foster care
3. Be a veteran of the Armed Forces or on active duty
4. Be a graduate or professional student
5. Be married
6. Have legal dependents
7. Be an emancipated minor or in legal guardianship
8. Be homeless

These criteria are straightforward and describe the majority of independent students on campus. So, what are your chances of becoming an Independent Student? A survey completed by the National Postsecondary Student Aid Study (NPSAS) found that, less than one-half of one percent of Independent Students were reclassified by a financial aid office dependency override

Realistically, for the majority of undergraduates, the only way to become an Independent Student is be 24 years old and or married. Attending college under these conditions is grueling, but millions of students do it every day.

Chapter Seventeen

Disability Services for College Students

Thousands of students with disabilities can now attend college with the expectation of success thanks to disability resource centers that are available on practically every campus in the United States. Centers offer <u>services</u>, such as tutoring and note taking, and <u>accommodations</u> such as Priority class registration and extra time to take a test. When choosing a community college or a four-year college, include the quality of the resources services available for your college-bound student in the decision-making process.

Sometimes parents look at college as one more battle and wonder whether it is worth the effort, while others push ahead knowing their son or daughter with a disability will have to work harder and hope their college-bound student will survive.

When parents begin their search for a college with a list of qualifiers in hand, college major, price, financial aid, campus safety, atmosphere, and distance from home to name a few, parents of students with a disability must also look for services that meet the unique needs of their son or daughter. The college must provide disability services for a wide range of student issues such as

> **Learning Disabilities** *related to Reading, (Dyslexia) Writing, (Dysgraphia) Mathematics, Auditory Processing, Visual Processing, Visual Spatial skills, and Processing Speed*
> **Attention Deficit Hyperactive *Disorder*** *(ADHD) relates to concentration, distractibility, organization, following directions, planning and organizing.*
> **Anxiety Disorder**, *Depression, Bipolar other psychiatric Disabilities*
> **Autism Spectrum Disorders** (ASD)

Mobility Disabilities, wheelchair accessibility
Deaf or hard of hearing
Blind or visually impaired
Medical Disabilities, *including Chronic Fatigue Syndrome,*
Fibromyalgia, Heart condition and Seizure Disorder

Once you have selected a few colleges, or even one, schedule a campus tour and make an appointment to visit the disability service center. It is important to get a first-hand impression of the staff and the services they offer that are specific to your child. Ask if your student is assigned a mentor or counselor, that is, one person he or she can go to with questions and concerns. Ask if they provide education and training for faculty.

But let's take a step back for a moment to the daunting task of taking the SATs or the ACT. In some cases, you can opt out, especially if you apply to a community college, but if the test is required, you have options.

College Board, which administers the Advanced Placement tests, PSAT and the SAT, offers Braille and large-print exams, extended time, use of a computer for essays and extra breaks. They will consider every parent request made to them for a documented disability. Discuss this with the high school guidance counselor, but don't be dissuaded if they don't feel an accommodation is needed

504 Plans
Your son or daughter may not have qualified for an Individualized Educational Program but may have received a 504 plan of accommodations. Section 504 of the Rehabilitation Act of 1973 defines qualified students as those with a physical or mental condition that substantially restricts one or more of the major life activities that include: Learning disabilities, Neurological conditions, Emotional or mental illnesses, Sense organ impairments, Organic brain syndromes, musculoskeletal impairments, Respiratory conditions, and Digestive ailments.

For the college to offer support services, you will need to provide them with documentation of the impairment. This frequently includes medical reports and treatment plans. Just don't bring in your request on the first day of school! They and you will need time to plan and prepare. Just so you know, colleges are not obligated to honor a high-school 504 plan and colleges do not use 504 plans. However, colleges are highly motivated to help students succeed and will provide whatever services they can to create a successful college experience.

As soon as your son or daughter has been accepted to college, and you have sent in your deposit, contact the disability service center to begin planning so every accommodation will be in place on the first day of school. Remember, you have already met with them during your campus visit and are satisfied they can provide the support necessary. The final plan may be nothing more than sitting in the front of the class and receiving extra time to take tests, but that should all be worked out before the first day of class. A variety of accommodations that may be available are

- Priority class registration
- Seating accommodations
- Testing Accommodations, extra time, quiet location, breaks
- Sound amplification aids, FM systems
- Speech to text software
- Note taking services
- Braille transcriptions
- Audio recording of lectures
- Tutoring

And, it wouldn't be a bad idea for your college student to let their professors know who they are, and that they will work hard to learn the material and earn good grades.

For all of this to fall into place, begin searching for colleges no later than your college-bound student's junior year. After finding a realistically priced school that offers sensible majors related to your student's strengths and interests, jump right over to the college's disability services to see what they have to offer.

Community colleges also offer a range of services for students with disabilities. My wife and I have a good friend with a son who is a successful college student. He works hard, receives tutoring, and earns good grades. His father taught him self-advocacy and the importance of sticking to your goals. For many reasons, students with disabilities do well in a community college, and the low cost of attending is a plus.

Advocacy vs. Privacy

Parents of students with disabilities have spent a lifetime seeking the best possible help and resources for their son or daughter. They have become generals overseeing the battle, directing the troops and pulling in reinforcements when necessary. They have become masters at cajoling, scolding, threatening and bribing to move their child along to an acceptable finish line. Sometimes parents are successful and sometimes there is more work to be done. Either way, once the college student has reached the age of 18, the age of majority, parents no longer command the battle field and are forcibly retired due to the age of the child.

In some cases, the-18-year-old will keep their parents informed ask their advice and make them part of their inner circle. In other cases, the 18-year-old, due to a streak of independence, or stubbornness, or disobedience, or even opposition, keep their own counsel with a closed door to outsiders (read parent here). For all these reasons, and for the sake of the student, an important part of a child's education is self-advocacy.

Self-Advocacy
Well first, if your son or daughter is receiving special-education services in high school, self-determination should be central to the course curriculum. Ask during a parent conference. Second...

Teaching your son or daughter to self-advocate is a long process that can best be taught by thoughtful and calm examples. The student must understand their disability, know their legal rights, learn what services are available, learn to firmly and positively ask for assistance, all with a smile on their face, of course. There may be self-advocacy programs in your state to provide assistance. There are books for sale on Amazon and possibly in your library, and there are websites to with information. One of the best is The *Center for Parent Information and Resources.*

For parents of a student with a disability, the first step is to know your rights under the law. The second step is to know what supports the college's disabilities service center provides for college students. And the third step is to teach your son or daughter the liberating experience that comes with the practice of self-advocacy.

Chapter Eighteen

Return on Investment

When it comes time to select a college, considering the school's return on investment (ROI) is an important step, but it gets complicated.

A common way to find the schools that give you the most for your money, is to let the print and electronic media do it for you. Forbes, Time, US News, Fortune, Petersons and various websites create an annual list of top schools in the United States. A lot of the information comes from PayScale, a robust website that calculates average salaries for every job in the workplace plus college graduates' early and mid-career income by school and major.

The annual US News and World Report Best Colleges, is an extensive listing read by thousands of people every year. MONEY's Best Colleges gets right to the point by displaying early career salaries and estimated cost with average financial aid. They and others use additional search criteria and a sophisticated formula to rank the best schools, which usually include Princeton, the University of Michigan, Harvard, Rice, and the University of California, Berkley in the top ten, but not necessarily in that order every year. These schools are great, but once those freshman slots are filled, there are another four million students looking for a school to call their own with anxious parents peering over their shoulder. Ditch the list

You can calculate a return on investment yourself by dividing the college's average Early Career Salary (posted by the college) by the expected four-year cost of attending. For example. The University of Massachusetts posts an average Early Career Salary of $46,600. The cost of attending is $30,000 a year for in-state students, or $120,000 total. Divide 46,600 by 120,000 and you get 0.388, or a 39 percent return on investment.

If that same student attended Worcester Polytechnic Institute, the average Early Career Salary is $65,300, but the four-year cost is $240,000. Divide 65,300 by 240,000 and you get 0.272 or a 27 percent return on investment. UMass clearly offers a better ROI, but the difference between the two beginning salaries is 18,700 dollars, or 40 percent. If that income variation is maintained until retirement, the WPI student can expect to earn a million dollars more than the UMass student.

Adding to the Formula's Accuracy
On the negative side, 1. the cost of attending college should include interest paid on a student loan. If you borrowed $6,000 a year or a total of $24,000, to be paid back over a ten-year period, the interest expense would be $6,617 if the money had been borrowed at 5.05 percent. 2. In in the UMass example, we assumed the student would graduate in four years, but 40 percent don't. Spending another year in college increases the original cost by 25 percent. 3. If you are an out-of-state student attending a public-college, the cost will be about one third higher. Enough of the bad news

On the plus side, most students do not pay the full cost of college, and your estimated financial aid should be deducted. Ninety percent of UMass students receive some assistance. The average aid package from Worcester Polytechnic Institute is $20,000. That alone brings their return on investment of 29 percent, up to 39 percent. For the fun of it, I picked on two schools in Massachusetts to create a comparison. I found all the information on the web, and you can do the same, when you select the schools you want to compare.

Calculating ROI can be fun, but let's get serious

In addition to early career salaries and cost of attending, parents need to look at Graduation Rates and Average Debt. I would rule out any school with a four-year graduation rate of less than 50 percent and would cautiously examine any school with an average student debt load of more than $24,000.

Another criteria used by MONEY and US News to find the top schools and ROI, was quality of education. And while this should be included in your search, it is a little more difficult to pin down. Of course, there is the old truth that a student will get out of college what they put in, but it would be nice to know that if the school or department, if not cutting edge, is at least on the top shelf, open to new ideas and ready to go. An interview with admissions and a department head would be helpful.

Select Schools by Department Quality

A college or university may be considered average by national standards, but a department or school within the university, may be of the same quality found in some of the top schools around the country. Conversely, an institution's great reputation does not necessarily carry over into every department. A quick look at department's focus, growth and the faculty biographies may tell the tale. Of course, this is of less value, if your student doesn't know what they want to do, but you can begin the winnowing process.

Consider their areas of interest and academic strengths. If academic strengths are equal, what do they prefer to study the least, because we all do what is easier, especially if we don't know what we want to do in the first place. Life careers have come and gone in jobs that were the least repugnant, for those who did not take the time to find something they truly enjoyed. You will need to translate your student's interest or sector-of-least-resistance into a generalized major that fits within the college academic structure. For example, which of these typical departments and majors found in colleges and universities can you cross off the list.

Biological sciences, Business, Communication and Journalism, Computer and Information science, Education, Engineering, Health professions and related, Psychology, Social science and history, Visual and Performing arts.

Of course, because there is a high demand for engineers, scientists, and other STEM majors, these fields are a safe investment, but they are not for everyone. If you have your heart on being a teacher or a social worker, two of the lowest paying professional jobs today, to make the return on investment work, you will have to attend a lower-cost public school with in-state tuition. Don't rule out spending the first two years in a quality community college.

Return on Investment of Time
There is another ROI that is important for college students, and that is, the return on investment of time spent. (ROITS). Which activities in a 24-hour cycle provide the best return for the amount of time they took to complete? Which activities produced the greatest amount of accomplishment and equanimity?

This was brought to mind recently, when our daughter decided to work on a school night. She is employed by a catering company and, in the past, only took jobs on the weekend or during school breaks. Well, working during the week, didn't work out. Her study and sleep schedule were crushed, and she spent the weekend catching up on both. Fortunately, this was a lesson well learned.

She now schedules her activities over reasonable periods of time to reach her goals. The key words here are schedule and goals, both of which are necessary for any one of us to move forward. Also important is to list, and then eliminate time wasting activities.

On The Lighter Side, Quora.com has invited people to submit lists of activities they believe constitute a waste of time, one of which included, reading lists of ways people waste time.

Chapter Nineteen

How Others Pay for College

While you are deciding how to pay for your son or daughter's college education, you might be interested to know and find some comfort in learning how the parents of twenty million other students are paying their college bills.

Twenty percent of families paid for college without seeking federal aid. The remaining 80 percent received grants, work-study, and scholarships. On average, parents paid 30 percent of college costs with their income and savings while students paid 12 percent with their income and savings[7]. Student can accomplish this with no reduction in federal aid by earning less than $6,560 a year. Even with college costing $35,000, the student could earn that 12 percent, or $4,200 during the summer. That means only 60 warm sunny workdays of an eight-hour shift at $9.00 an hour not counting tips. Students can earn the full $35,000 if they sign on as a cook in an Alaskan crab fishing boat.

Students and parents also took out loans, but less than in the past. Loans paid 24 percent of costs in four-year public colleges and about 30 percent of costs in four-year private colleges. Interestingly, one third of families who took out loans assumed financial aid and scholarships would cover the cost of college and did not expect to borrow money. You can narrow this information down to an individual state or college by checking college guides such as Fiske and Peterson or go online to The Institute for College Access and Success (www.ticas.org) web page which reports the average student debt of every state and college.

Many students and families are finding ways to decrease college expenses. Sixty-nine percent of students opted for in-state schools and lower tuitions. Sixty-one percent are living closer to home or with relatives, so they can commute. Forty-two percent are living with a roommate, and twenty-eight percent are accelerating the pace of coursework to complete their degree in less than four years. During a visit to a large university, a chemistry professor informed two-hundred parents that chemistry majors require five or more years to complete their bachelor's degree due to the number of courses they are required to complete. My wife and I agreed if a university can't get its act together enough to allow a student to earn a bachelor's degree in four years we should run, not walk to the nearest exit.

After using up grants, scholarships, work-study and student loans, how do we pay the balance owed? Here are five ways, not including check, cash, gold, or blood.

1. Pay for college with parent and student income and assets. These include money from your paycheck and savings in any form.

2. Pay for college with a Home-Equity Line of Credit, (Not a Home Equity Loan) A home-equity line of credit to pay for college offers the following benefits.

    a. You pay no interest until you write the check.
    b. The interest rate is usually low
    c. You can deduct interest paid from your taxes creating a lower AGI and with a second home, the loaned amount reduces equity in property reducing reportable assets. The downside? You are borrowing money at a variable rate that could increase over time. Pay these loans off quickly.

3. Pay for college with a Margin Loan
College costs can be paid with a loan from a stock market margin account. You don't touch your stocks allowing them to follow the market while reducing your net-worth which should increase your

financial aid package. Remember a margin loan is a bet that the value of your stock will increase enough to offset the amount of interest you are paying on the loan.

4. Pay for college with a Credit Card

Most colleges and universities allow you to pay tuition with a credit card, but they will charge a transaction fee in excess of the points you might earn, so you generally pay more in the end. The additional danger is that you fail to pay off your card at the end of the month, incurring interest rate charges that will land you in the poorhouse well before your son or daughter graduates.

5. Tuition Payment Plans

Many colleges offer a monthly payment plan, which may be easier on your budget. Other colleges offer a tuition freeze if you pay the four years up front. This could save you money depending upon the amount of interest you have to pay if you borrowed the money, or the interest you would lose by pulling money out of savings. I'm guessing if you could afford to pay four years of college in advance you wouldn't be filling out FAFSA or reading this book.

Lost Opportunity Cost

Sometimes it is better to borrow money and pay interest than lose the opportunity to earn a profit on your stock market holdings which you will never get back if you sell them. For example, when calculating this out, take the long view. How will those stocks perform in the next ten years? Which will be greater, the loss of stock growth or the cost of a loan? Put on your prognosticator cap and take out your calculator.

Chapter Twenty

Taking a Gap Year

Thousands of students take a gap year after high-school graduation before entering college by finding something to do on their own or participating in an agency sponsored program at home or abroad. Completing a gap year can produce a deeper level of maturity and a broader perspective on life that college administrators appreciate, while the student benefits from a stronger sense of personal identity and the ability to view his or her major studies in a wider context than their peers. It's a good deal for everyone, if you've got the time and the money.

The Rest of the Story
There is no one to keep track of how many students take a gap year between high school and college, or the many reasons for doing so, or even how many take more than one year before continuing their education, but there are enough, that a gap-year industry has grown up to service these students and their parents.

In my day, as parents are prone to say, a typical homegrown remedy for students unable to decide whether to go to college, would be to spend a year working in a sweatshop and taking one or two courses at a community college and this was usually enough to encourage or discourage the student from soldiering-on to complete a two or four-year college degree.

Same Old, Same Old.
Going to college right after high school is a ratcheting up of what students have been doing for the last 12 years. They'll only be doing more of the same, albeit at a quicker pace, and from a point of view (the student's) that has changed very little over the years. On the other hand, doing something completely different in a gap year opens the mind to opportunities that would otherwise remain hidden from view. This insight increases the value of a college

education from taking a course to get a grade, to accumulating knowledge for the sake of knowledge, which adds considerably to the meaning and relevance of the student's education, future vocation and personal fulfillment.

Not Everyone Moves On

We should say from the start, not everyone moves on to college following their gap year and not every high school graduate needs to go to a four-year college. Many do well by attending a two-year trade school, or technology college, or going to work for a large company with opportunities for advancement. Some of these companies will pay a portion of a student's tuition if they show promise and earn good grades. Other students do well joining a branch of the military that pays tuition for selected college courses and an eventual degree.

Give Me a Break

For the thousands of students determined to earn a college degree, **but not yet**, there are some life-changing reasons to take an organized, coordinated, goal-driven gap-year, not the least of which is entering the next phase of life with a worldlier perspective sprinkled with a touch of reality. And fortunately for these students, there are hundreds of opportunities to take a full or half-gap year participating in programs abroad or closer to home in an area of interest they would like to explore.

However

Before planning your round-the-world trip to far flung locations, captivating cultures while chatting up the locals for bargains, you still must work on your high-school GPA, take your SAT or ACT test, apply to first and second-choice schools and be accepted. Don't wait until you are in your gap year to apply and don't expect your gap-year experience to get you into college. Most colleges recognize the advantage of a gap year, like to have those students on campus and offer a deferment while they accrue those life-changing experiences, but before all of that, the student has to be accepted.

Where to Begin
While the gap-year student should consider the three evaluative queries below, parents should cling onto them like a life-raft in a storm. Since my daughter did not put us through a gap-year experience, I can only imagine what gap-year parents feel, but you should find comfort and a degree of sanity by evaluating the proposed gap-year within the framework of these three questions.

1. Will the student be challenged with learning opportunities outside a normal classroom setting?
2. Will the student be with peers taking a gap year that are also seeking learning opportunities in a safe environment?
3. Will there be adult mentors available to provide guidance, consistency, challenging ideas, perspective and protection?

How to Proceed
Unless you have a gap-year experience mapped out, the first thing I would do as parent, is go online and check out the **Gap Year Association** website. Yes, there is one. Their primary mission is to make others aware of gap-year opportunities and to accredit gap-year programs which they list on their website.

You will find that many of these programs run for a few months or less and many of them take place overseas. Another website, **GoAbroad.com** will lead you to many opportunities to volunteer, study and experience life in another country. They also offer many summer programs. So, if your son or daughter is still a freshman, and you want to broaden their perspective without taking a year off after high school, there are program opportunities that do not eat into their academic schedule. **Our daughter traveled to Ireland and Greece with other students, fulfilling her gap-year wanderlust before high school graduation.**

Want to talk to someone first hand? Attend one of the USA **Gap Year Fairs** that are held around the country. If you can talk your school into hosting a gap-year fair, they will come to you. Fairs are most often held in the fall.

One of the most comprehensive websites for students going abroad is the **Council on International Educational Exchange** (CIEE). Click on "Programs" and a map displays program locations around the world, which are divided into three major areas: 1 Language and Culture, 2 Service and Leadership and 3 Global Internship.

My suggestion to parents is this. If you believe there is even a remote possibility that your son or daughter might want to take a gap year, get a jump on the process by becoming familiar with the options. If nothing else, you might find some vacation spots that have escaped your attention. And one other thing. If your student thinks they would like to spend a couple of months in one country or another eradicating hunger or increasing the water supply, they may need to increase their time line.

Chapter Twenty-one

How to Use the Website
www.survivingthecostofcollege.com

The book's companion website is designed to keep you organized and provide you with the resources to make smart college choices

Website Organization

First Step. Get Organized.
  1. Download and Print College Preparation To-Do List. Tracks activities and deadlines that begin in freshman year

Second Step. **Find and Finance** your College Choice
  2. Planning Resources. Best colleges for your college-bound
  3. Financial Resources. Grants, scholarships, loans

Third Step
  4. College Selection Provides organized process to compare twelve Key Indicators for comparing and selecting a college. See how Mary Smith compared the results of four different colleges. Also includes College visit Evaluation forms and College Selection checklist
  5. Student Applications. Links to SAT, FAFSA, CSS Profile and Common Applications. Download applications to see what they look like before you go online.

Education Alerts. Provides list of changes affecting colleges, scams, and warning signs to heed.

College Insight. Monthly columns covering educational and financial information for parents. Over 70 columns are archived.

Book Resources. Provides all the forms, files and links used in the book. They are listed under the chapter in which they are referred.

Forms and Tables

EFC Formula Worksheet and Tables A1 -7

In Chapter Five, Rules of the game, Mary Smith's Expected Family Contribution (EFC) was calculated using the federal government EFC FORMULA: Dependent Student form.

The next two pages contain a blank form that you may use to calculate your EFC. The whole process takes about ten minutes.

To complete the calculations look-up tables are required. These are printed on the following pages. The look-up tables information is crucial as those numbers lower your Expected Family Contribution.

You can also download the most recent version of these forms from our website. Go to the Financial Planning page.

Good Luck.

PARENTS' INCOME			AVAILABLE INCOME	
1. Parents' Adjusted Gross Income			Total income from line 7	
2a. Parent 1 income			Subtract Total allowances from line 14	
2b. Parent 2 income			15. **AVAILABLE INCOME**	
Total of parent #1 & #2 income				
3. Parents' Taxable income Tax filers enter from line 1 Non-tax filers enter line 2			**PARENTS CONTRIBUTION FROM ASSETS**	
4. Total untaxed income and benefits FAFSA question #94			16. Cash savings and checking	
5. Total income (L3/4)			17. Net worth of investments	
6. Total additional financial information FAFSA question #93.			18. Net worth of business or	
7. **Total Income**. Line 5 - line 6.			19. Adjusted net worth of business/ farm **TABLE A4**	
			20. **Net Worth**. Sum lines 16,17 & 19	
ALLOWANCES AGAINST PARENT'S INCOME			21. education savings and assets Use **TABLE A5**	
8. Federal income tax paid			22. Discretionary net worth L20 - L21	
9. Tax allowance. **TABLE A 1** +			23. Asset conversion rate	.12
10. Parent 1 social security **TABLE A2**			**24. CONTRIBUTION FROM ASSETS**	
11. Parent 2 social security **TABLE A2**				
12. Income protection **TABLE A3**			**PARENTS' CONTRIBUTION**	
13. Employment expense Allowance:			**AVAILABLE INCOME** from line 15	
			CONTRIBUTION FOR ASSETS from line 24	
			25. Adjusted Available Income (AAI)	
			26. Total parents' contribution AAI Calculate using **TABLE A6**	
			27. Number in college	
			28.**PARENTS' CONTRIBUTION** Divide by number in line 27	
14. **TOTAL ALLOWANCES** 8 through 13 =				

STUDENT INCOME		STUDENT'S CONTRIBUTION	
29. Adjusted Gross Income		45. Cash, savings & checking	
30. Income earned from work		46. Net worth of investments	
31. Taxable income Tax filers enter amount from line 29 Non-tax filers enter from line 30		47. Net worth of business and/ or investment farm	
32. Total untaxed income and benefits See FAFSA question # 45		48. **Net worth** Sum lines 45 - 47	
33. Total taxable and untaxed income		49. Assessment rate	0.20
34. Total additional financial information FAFSA question # 44		50. STUDENT'S ASSETS CONTRIBUTION	
35. TOTAL INCOME Line 33 minus line 34			
		EXPECTED FAMILY CONTRIBUTION	
ALLOWANCES AGAINST STUDENT INCOME		**PARENTS' CONTRIBUTION** from line 28	
36. U.S. income tax paid last year		**STUDENT'S CONTRIBUTION FROM AI** from line 44	
37. State allowance **TABLE A7**		**STUDENT'S CONTRIBUTION FROM ASSETS** from line 50	
38. Social Security allow **TABLE A2**		**51. EXPECTED FAMILY CONTRIBUTION**	
39. Income protection allowance			
40. Allowance for parents' negative Adjusted Available Income. If line 25 is negative, enter line 25 as a positive number. If line 25 is zero or positive, enter zero here.			
41. **TOTAL ALLOWANCES**			
STUDENT'S CONTRIBUTION FROM INCOME			
Total Income from line 35 above			
Total allowances from line 41 above			
42. **Available income (AI)**			
43. Assessment of AI	.50		
44. STUDENT'S CONTRIBUTION FROM AI =			

Table A1: State and Other Tax Allowance
For EFC Formula A Worksheet (Parents only)

STATE	INCOME 0-14,999	15000 +	STATE	INCOME 0-14,999	15000 +
Alabama	3%	2%	Missouri	4%	3%
Alaska	2%	1%	Montana	5%	4%
American Samoa	2%	1%	Nebraska	5%	4%
Arizona	4%	3%	Nevada	2%	1%
Arkansas	4%	3%	New Hampshire	5%	4%
California	7%	6%	New Jersey	9%	8%
Canada Provinces	2%	1%	New Mexico	3%	2%
Colorado	4%	3%	New York	9%	8%
Connecticut	8%	7%	North Carolina	5%	4%
Delaware	5%	4%	North Dakota	2%	1%
District Columbia	7%	6%	Mariana	2%	1%
Fed. Micronesia	2%	1%	Ohio	5%	4%
Florida	3%	2%	Oklahoma	3%	2%
Georgia	5%	4%	Oregon	7%	6%
Guam	2%	1%	Palau	2%	1%
Hawaii	5%	4%	Pennsylvania	5%	4%
Idaho	5%	4%	Puerto Rico	2%	1%
Illinois	6%	5%	Rhode Island	7%	6%
Indiana	4%	3%	South Carolina	5%	4%
Iowa	5%	4%	South Dakota	2%	1%
Kansas	5%	4%	Tennessee	2%	1%
Kentucky	5%	4%	Texas	3%	2%
Louisiana	3%	2%	Utah	5%	4%
Maine	6%	5%	Vermont	6%	5%
Marshall Islands	2%	1%	Virgin Islands	2%	1%
Maryland	8%	7%	Virginia	6%	5%
Massachusetts	6%	5%	Washington	3%	2%
Mexico	2%	1%	West Virginia	3%	2%
Michigan	4%	3%	Wisconsin	7%	6%
Minnesota	6%	5%	Wyoming	2%	1%
Mississippi	3%	2%	OTHER	2%	1%

Table A2: Social Security Tax

Calculate separately the Social Security tax of father, mother and of student

Earned Income*	Social Security Tax
$0 - $118,500 equals	7.65% of income
$118,501 + equals	$9,065.25 + 1.45% of amount over 118,500

Table A3: Income Protection Allowance

Number in household	Number of college students in household				
	1	2	3	4	5
2	17,840	14,790	0	0	0
3	22,220	19,180	16,310	0	0
4	27,440	24,390	21,350	18,300	0
5	32,380	29,320	26,290	23,240	20,200
6	37,870	34,820	31,780	28,730	25,690

Note: For each additional family member. Add $4,180.
        For each additional college student subtract $2,970.

Table A4: Business/Farm Net Worth

If the net worth of business is:	Then the adjusted net worth is--
Less than $1	$0
$1 to $125,000	40% of net worth of business/farm
$125,001 to $380,000	$50,000 + 50% of net worth over 125,000
$380,001 to $635,000	$177,500 + 60% of net worth over 380,000
$635,000 or more	$330,500 + 100% of net worth over 635,000

Age of older parent	Allowance 2 parents	Allowance 1 parent	Age of older parent	Allowance 2 parents	Allowance 1 parent
Table A5 Savings and Asst Protection Allowance					
25 Or less	$0	$0	45.........	$17,400	$8,800
26.........	1,000	500	46.........	17,800	900
27.........	2,100	1,100	47.........	18,300	9,200
28.........	3,100	1,600	48.........	18,700	9,400
29.........	4,100	2,100	49.........	19,200	9,700
30.........	5,200	2,600	50.........	19,700	9,900
31.........	6,200	3,200	51.........	20,200	10,100
32.........	7,200	3,700	52.........	20,700	10,400
33.........	8,300	4,200	53.........	21,300	10,600
34.........	9,300	4,700	54.........	21,800	10,900
35.........	10,300	5,300	55.........	22,400	11,100
36.........	11,400	5,800	56.........	23,000	11,400
37.........	12,400	6,300	57.........	23,700	11,700
38.........	13,400	6,800	58.........	24,300	12,000
39.........	14,500	7,400	59.........	25,000	12,300
40.........	15,500	7,900	60.........	25,700	12,600
41.........	15,900	8,100	61.........	26,400	12,900
42.........	16,300	8,300	62.........	27,200	13,200
43.........	16,600	8,500	63.........	27,900	13,600
44.........	17,000	8,600	64.........	28,800	13,900
			65 or over	29,600	14,300

Table A6 Parents Contribution from AAI	
less than $3,409	$750
3,409 to 15,900	22% of AAI
15,901 to 20,000	$3,498 + 25% of AAI over 15,900
20,001 to 24,100	$4,523 + 29% of AAI over 20,000
24,101 to 28,200	$5,712 + 34% of AAI over 24,100
28,201 to 32,200	$7,106 + 40% of AAI over 28,200
31,701 32,201 or more	$8,706 + 47% of AAI over 32,200

Table A7: State and Other Tax Allowance
For EFC Formula A Worksheet **Students only**

Alabama	2%	Missouri	3%
Alaska	0%	Montana	3%
American Samoa	1%	Nebraska	3%
Arizona	2%	Nevada	1%
Arkansas	3%	New Hampshire	1%
California	5%	New Jersey	4%
Canada & Provinces	1%	New Mexico	2%
Colorado	3%	New York	6%
Connecticut	5%	North Carolina	4%
Delaware	3%	North Dakota	1%
District of Columbia	5%	Mariana Island	1%
Federated States of	1%	Ohio	3%
Florida	1%	Oklahoma	2%
Georgia	3%	Oregon	5%
Guam	1%	Palau	1%
Hawaii	4%	Pennsylvania	3%
Idaho	3%	Puerto Rico	1%
Illinois	3%	Rhode Island	3%
Indiana	3%	South Carolina	3%
Iowa	3%	South Dakota	1%
Kansas	3%	Tennessee	1%
Kentucky	4%	Texas	1%
Louisiana	2%	Utah	3%
Maine	4%	Vermont	3%
Marshall Islands	1%	Virgin Islands	1%
Maryland	5%	Virginia	4%
Massachusetts	4%	Washington	1%
Mexico	1%	West Virginia	2%
Michigan	3%	Wisconsin	4%
Minnesota	4%	Wyoming	1%
Mississippi	2%	Other	2%

Index

Index

Author's Page

Bob Sherman holds a master's degree in education from West Virginia University and for the last five years has been researching educational issues, college finance and federal funding, writing a column for the website: www.survivingthecostofcollege.com

He spent 34 years as a public and private school administrator budgeting, planning and supervising programs for special education and gifted students. He also managed two clinical teams that diagnosed and developed treatment plans for educational and psychological school-related issues. Following retirement, he developed and licensed software for administrators and teachers to track and report student programs and progress for schools in Rhode Island, Connecticut and Massachusetts. He also designed software for a public-school business department that recorded and reported all revenues and expenses while tracking purchases and inventory. Later, he developed software for a private company to track product inventory, costs and sales, gross and net profit. During this time, he also owned and operated a real estate company that invested in and managed rental properties.

As treasurer of the Smith-Appleby House Museum and Smithfield Historical Society in Rhode Island he manages the finances, reporting, tax preparation and IRS reporting for the non-profit corporation.

When not working, Bob's activities include: running, tennis, boating, and skiing. His wife, Lisa, is a second-grade teacher and certified yoga instructor. They live at home with their cat wondering what their college-student daughter is up to today.